DISCARD

THE HOMES OF DONEGAL

SEAN McMAHON

MERCIER PRESS

Mercier Press
PO Box 5 5 French Church Street Cork
16 Hume Street Dublin 2

First published 1995

© Introduction Sean McMahon 1995
© All translations from Irish and Latin Sean McMahon, unless
otherwise stated.
The acknowledgements page is an extension of this copyright
notice.

A CIP record for this book is available from the British Library.

ISBN 1 85635 101 7

10 9 8 7 6 5 4 3 2 1

Set by Richard Parfrey
Cover design by Brian Finnegan
Printed in Ireland by ColourBooks Baldoyle Dublin 13

For Shane and Ciana

Subtleman: And how do you intend to live?
Teague: By eating, dear joy, fen I can get it; and by sleeping
               when I can get none; tish the fashion of Ireland.

The Twin Rivals by George Farquhar
(b. Raphoe 1677; d. London 1707)

Acknowledgements

For permission to reproduce copyright material, the Publishers are grateful to the following:

Waltons Ltd for 'The Homes of Donegal' by Sean MacBride; Mercier Press Ltd for the extracts from: *Caisleán Óir* by 'Máire'; *An Beál Bocht* by Myles na gCopaleen; *Islanders* by Peadar O'Donnell; *The Islands of Ireland* by T. H. Mason; *The Secret Places of Donegal* by John M. Feehan; Pat the Cope Gallagher for the extract from *My Story* by Paddy the Cope Gallagher; the estate of Flann O'Brien and A M Heath & Co Ltd for the extract from *The Poor Mouth*; Andrew Lownie for the extract from *A House of Children* by Joyce Cary; Peter Razzell for 'Dedication' and 'Going Home' by Patrick MacGill; Faber and Faber Ltd for lines from 'Western Landscape' by Louis MacNeice from *The Collected Poems of Louis MacNeice* edited by E. R. Dobbs; Gill and Macmillan for 'The Horsemen of Aileach'' by Alice Milligan; 'Eithne' and 'Farewell to Donegal' by Seumas MacManus; John Boyd for 'Towards Donegal'; Mrs Eileen O'Sullivan for 'Dawn on Inishtrahull' by D. J. O'Sullivan; 'Lough Derg' by kind permission of the trustees of the Estate of Patrick Kavanagh c/o Peter Fallon, Literary Agent, Loughcrew, Oldcastle, Co Meath, Ireland; Allen Figgis & Co for extract from *The Way That I Went* by Robert Lloyd Praeger; Cló Iar-Chonnachta Teo for 'Anseo ag Stáisiún Chaiseal na gCorr' from *Homecoming / An Bealach 'na Bhaile* by Cathal Ó Searcaigh; Gabriel Fitzmaurice for his translation of 'Anseo ag Stáisiún Chaiseal na gCorr'; Séamus Ó Cnaimhsí for the extract from 'An Chéad Meisce agus an Meisce Dheireanach' le Seán Bán Mac Meanman; the extract from *My Cousin Justin* by Margaret Barrington reprinted by permission of the Peters Fraser and Dunlop Group Ltd.

The Publishers would be pleased to be notified of and to make good any errors or omissions in the above acknowledgements.

CONTENTS

LABHRAÍTEAR GAEILGE ANSEO

PROUD INISHOWEN

HIGHLAND AND ISLANDS

SONGS AND STORIES

HERE AND THERE

FARE YE WELL

INTRODUCTION

Donegal is one of a handful of Irish counties which has virtually universal approbation. Dubliners and Belfastmen feel equally at home there and Derry people unreasonably if understandably regard their city as its capital. It is famous for its scenery, its beaches, its islands and, in a different sense, its roads and weather. Its roads with a few European exceptions are narrow and often twisted and its weather, as a rule, may be judged by the wintry smile of the met men as they say, 'Especially in the northwest . . . ' or 'Except in the northwest . . . ' Yet the rain and the wind and the mist do not seem to matter. There is an unmatchable interior warmth of hospitality while it pours, and breathtaking beauty as Errigal, Muckish, Slieve League or Slieve Snaght break through the clouds again into the sunshine.

It is a big county by Irish standards: from Rossan Point to Inishowen Head is a crow-flight of eighty miles, Derry to Dungloe forty-two and the journey by road from its most northerly point at Malin Head to its border with Leitrim at the mouth of the Drowes River is more than a hundred miles. It has some of the best and some of the worst land in Ireland and a mixture of scenery that varies from the lunar to English Home Counties.

As will be clear I am not a disinterested witness – no DA would allow me on the jury – and this compilation is a kind of tribute for the many years of pleasure that the county has given me, not least that as I shave each morning I can look at its lovely hills. No anthology, however, can do full justice to it and this is a mere indication of the richness that is to be found there and of the pleasure it has ever given to the visitor. As with all such trawls the favourite pieces left out or the authors unincluded will annoy many who have a kind of Donegal book already in their heads. I can only say in exculpation that the choice was personal and, I hope, not too idiosyncratic.

I am indebted to Seán MacBride for gracious permission to use as title the name of one of Donegal's best known songs, and to Réamann Ó Gallchóir and Frank D'Arcy for advice and help.

THE PRIDE OF ALL

The Best County
from *The Way that I Went*
Robert Lloyd Praeger

Robert Lloyd Praeger was born in Holywood, Co Down, in 1865 and became a civil engineer with an intense interest in geology. He served as head of the National Library, wrote many books on botany and died in Belfast in 1953.

If you ask what is the best county in Ireland to walk in, I reply, Donegal (or Tirconnell, *Tír Conaill*, Connell's country), to give it its ancient name). I express no opinion as regards motoring, for if one can traverse a county from end to end in a couple of hours, it is countries (or at least provinces) not counties that should be the unit. But for the wise motorist who can restrain its ardour, and uses his car in order to see the country instead of leaving it behind, the walking choice holds good, and Donegal comes first. I choose it because there is nowhere else where the beauties of hill and dale, lake and rock, sea and bog, pasture and tillage, are so intimately and closely interwoven, so that every turn of the road opens new prospects, and every hill-crest fresh combinations of these delightful elements. But the best kind of car for Donegal would be one whose maximum speed is ten miles an hour, and which needs to rest at frequent intervals.

Donegal (*Dún na nGall*, fort of the foreigners) owes its topography to very ancient happenings. In times so remote that scarcely any portion of the present Ireland was in existence, the rocks of this area were crumpled together and thrown into ridges and hollows running north-east and south-west; the features thus impressed upon the region millions of years ago still persist. Look at a geological map and a map showing elevation, and you will see how intimately related are the rocks with the modelling of the county; compare these with a general map, and you will note how human movement within the area, as demonstrated by the trend of roads and railways, obeys the ancient disposition. Communication is easy along the lines of folding, but railways and highways achieve a north-west direction with difficulty, and to the accompaniment of much clambering and twisting. Londonderry and Strabane, the natural centres of distribution, transmit their merchandise – human or otherwise – to the Atlantic coast only by devious meanderings among mountain ridges.

In the inland portions of Donegal the hills are lower, the old foldings less pronounced, and there is much fertile land and some fine streams; this region has many pleasing prospects, but little of the charm of rock and bog and lake which characterises the remainder. A maritime zone fifteen miles wide, embracing about half the county, includes all the places which make Donegal beloved by the tourist and the naturalist; the landward part, drained mostly by the Foyle and its tributary streams, is welcome mainly as a means of passage to the wilder country beyond. A further glace at a geological map shows a prevalence of quartzite – a hard and intractable rock – in the north-western half of Donegal: and mountain-climbing there confirms the deduction that most of the higher hills – Slieve Snacht, Muckish, the beautiful white cone of Errigal, Slievatooey, Slieve League, for example – are great humps of this resistant material, which have remained while the softer rocks around them have slowly crumbled under the attacks of rain and wind, and for a while of ice. The great area of schists which occupies the south-eastern half of Donegal and extends far across Derry and Tyrone shows no outlines equally bold, though the Sperrin Mountains rise to over 2000 feet. This wilder north-western region, which gives

Donegal its fame, is extensive, measuring over eighty miles from Inishowen Head to Malinmore Head (which has nothing to do with Malin Head), fronting the ocean all the way; and not a mile of it is dull. It is sown with mountains, gashed by deep rocky inlets of the sea, studded with lakes; where neither sea nor lake nor mountain holds possession, little fields struggle for mastery with rock and heather. Of the features that go to make a region lovely, woodland alone is rare in Donegal: exposure to Atlantic storms inhibits natural tree-growth save where shelter is found. In such places vegetation is luxuriant; not only native trees but half-hardy exotic shrubs flourish here in a manner recalling the wonderful gardens of Kerry. Indeed, the two hundred miles or more that separate these two extremities of Ireland cause very little change so far as climate is concerned. Both Kerry and Donegal have over-abundance of rain and wind, and there is suprisingly little difference as regards temperature. The January isotherm of 42° Fahrenheit which crosses Donegal, crosses also the northern end of Kerry; and Kerry is only one degree warmer in July than is the most northerly county in Ireland.

Dedication

Patrick MacGill

Patrick MacGill was born near Glenties in 1890. His novels Ch*ildren of the Dead End* (1914) and *The Rat Pit* (1915) were based upon his own experiences as a labourer in Scotland. He died in the USA in 1963. This poem is a foreword to his *Songs of Donegal*.

I speak with a proud tongue of the people who were
And the people who are,
The worthy of Ardara, the Rosses and Inishkeel,
My kindred –
The people of the hills and dark-haired passes
My neighbours on the lift of the brae
In the lap of the valley.

To them Slainthe!

I speak of the old men,
The wrinkle-rutted,
Who dodder about foot-weary –
For their day is as the day that has been and is no more –
Who warm their feet by the fire,
And recall memories of the times that are gone;
Who kneel in the lamplight and pray
For the peace that has been theirs –
And who beat one dry-veined hand against another
Even in the sun –
For the coldness of death is on them.

I speak of the old women
Who danced to yesterday's fiddle
And dance no longer.
They sit in a quiet place and dream
And see visions
Of what is to come,
Of their issue,
Which has blossomed to manhood and womanhood –
And seeing thus
They are happy
For the day that was leaves no regrets
And peace is theirs
And perfection.

I speak of the strong men
Who shoulder their burdens in the hot day,
Who stand in the market-place
And bargain in loud voices,
Showing their stock to the world.
Straight the glance of their eyes –
Broad-shouldered,
Supple.
Under their feet the holms blossom,
The harvest yields.
And their path is of prosperity.

I speak of the women,
Strong-hipped, full-bosomed,
Who drive the cattle to graze at dawn,
Who milk the cows at dusk.
Grace in their homes,
And in the crowded ways

Modest and seemly –
Mothers of children!

I speak of the children
Of the many townlands,
Blossoms of the Bogland,
Flowers of the Valley,
Who know not yesterday, nor to-morrow,
And are happy,
The pride of those who have begot them.
And thus it is,
Ever and always,
In Ardara, the Rosses and Inishkeel –
Here, as elsewhere,
The Weak, the Strong, and the Blossoming –
And thus my kindred.

To them Slainthe.

Sheephaven
From 'Western Landscape'
Louis MacNeice

Louis MacNeice was born in Belfast in 1907, the son of the man who
afterwards became Bishop of Connor, and had a double fame as poet and
writer/producer for the BBC. He died in 1963.

In doggerel and stout let me honour this country
Though the air is so soft that it smudges the words
And herds of great clouds find the gaps in the fences

Of chance preconceptions and foam-quoits on rock-points
At once hit and miss, hit and miss.
So the kiss of the past is narcotic, the ocean
Lollingly lullingly over-insidiously
Over and under crossing the eyes
And docking the queues of the teetotum consciousness
Proves and disproves what it wants.
For the western climate is Lethe,
The smoky taste of cooking on turf is lotus,
There are affirmation and abnegation together
From the broken bog with its veins of amber water,
From the distant headland, a sphinx's fist, that barely grips
    the sea,
From the taut-necked donkey's neurotic-asthmatic-erotic
    lamenting,
From the heron in trance and in half-mourning,
From the mitred mountain weeping shale.

The Homes of Donegal
Sean MacBride

Sean MacBride was born in Cruit Island off Kincasslagh in 1902 and became
a teacher. He has written several songs and stories and a novel about island
life called *Herring out the Bay.*

I've just stepped in to see you all,
I'll only stay a while;
I want to see how you're getting on,
I want to see you smile;
I'm happy to be back again,

I greet you big and small
For there's no place else on earth
Just like the Homes of Donegal.

I always see the happy faces,
Smiling at the door,
The kettle swinging on the crook
As I step up the floor;
And soon the taypot's fillin' up
Me cup that's far from small
For your hearts are like your mountains
In the Homes of Donegal.
To see your homes at parting day
Of that I never tire
And hear the porridge bubblin'
In a big pot on the fire.
The lamp alight, the dresser bright,
The big clock on the wall,
O, a sight serene celestial scene
In the Homes of Donegal.

I long to sit along with you
And while away the night
With tales of yore and fairy lore
Beside your fires so bright
And then to see prepared for me
A shake-down by the wall;
There's repose for weary wanderers
In the Homes of Donegal.

Outside the night winds shriek and howl;
Inside there's peace and calm.

The picture on the wall up there's
Our Saviour with a lamp,
The hope of wandering sheep like me
And all who rise and fall.
There's a touch of heavenly love around
The Homes of Donegal.

A tramp I am and a tramp I've been,
A tramp I'll always be.
Me father tramped, me mother tramped;
Sure trampin's bred in me.
If some there are my ways disdain
And won't have me at all,
Sure I'll always find a welcome
In the Homes of Donegal.

The time has come and I must go;
I bid you all adieu.
The open highway calls me forth
To do the things I do
And when I'm trampin' far away
I'll hear your voices call
And please God I'll soon return unto
The Homes of Donegal.

Towards Donegal

John Boyd

John Boyd was born in 1912 in Belfast and worked as a teacher and BBC
producer. He has written several plays and is on the board of the Lyric
Theatre.

The halo of sun now holds the hills
of Donegal, while here I stand
watching the gathering cloud that falls
over those hills nightly, like a fan
unfolded in an orient tale.
I have never known those lost hills
nor their people; nor the soft tongue
spoken there; nor the silence that falls
with the soldered sun; nor the valleys along
the crackling coast now bare of sail
or smoke of ship. Yet I can tell
my children legends woven there
in winter's woe: and telling feel
the spell in the wondering stare
of candid eyes captured by the living tale.

CHILDHOOD

The Fairies
(A Child's Song)
William Allingham

William Allingham was born in Ballyshannon in 1824 and served for many years as a customs officer. He wrote this poem one January day in Killybegs. His latter years were spent in England though when he died in 1889 he was taken home for burial in Ballyshannon.

Up the airy mountain,
    Down the rushy glen,
We daren't go a-hunting
    For fear of little men;
Wee folk, good folk,
    Trooping all together;
Green jacket, red cap,
    And white owl's feather!

Down along the rocky shore
    Some make their home –
They live on crispy pancakes
    Of yellow tide-foam;
Some in the reeds
    Of the black mountain lake,
With frogs for their watch-dogs,
    All night awake.

High on the hill-top
    The old King sits;
He is now so old and grey

He's nigh lost his wits.
With a bridge of white mist
    Columbkill he crosses,
On his stately journey
    From Slieveleague to Rosses;
Or going up with music
    On cold starry nights,
To sup with the Queen
    Of the gay Northern lights.

They stole little Bridget
    For seven years long;
When she came down again
    Her friends were all gone.
They took her lightly back,
    Between the night and morrow;
They thought that she was fast asleep,
    But she was dead with sorrow.
They have kept her ever since
    Deep within the lake,
On a bed of flag-leaves,
    Watching till she wake.

By the craggy hill-side,
    Though the mosses bare,
They have planted thorn-trees
    For pleasure here and there.
Is any man so daring
    As dig one up in spite,
He shall find the sharpest thorns
    In his bed at night.

Up the airy mountain,
    Down the rushy glen,
We daren't go a-hunting
    For fear of little men;
Wee folk, good folk,
    Trooping all together;
Green jacket, red cap,
    And white owl's feather!

Four Ducks on a Pond
William Allingham

Four ducks on a pond,
A grass-bank beyond,
A blue sky of spring
White birds on the wing:
What a little thing
To remember for years –
To remember with tears!

Hired
From *My Story*
Paddy the Cope Gallagher

Paddy the Cope was born in Cleendra near Dungloe in 1871 and after discovering the cooperative movement as an labourer in Scotland determined to foster the idea at home. The result was the Templecrone Cooperative, an end to gombeenism and a permanent nickname. He died in Dungloe in 1964.

The Rosses is on the west coast of County Donegal, Ireland. There are one hundred and nine townlands in the Rosses. Cleendra is one of them. Cleendra lies on sloping ground facing the Atlantic. I often heard that Neil Og's house is the highest house in Ireland, and many a pleasant evening I spent there listening to Neil Og and his sister, Maire, telling stories. They are both dead long ago. Whenever I visit Cleendra, and look up at the ruins of the grand old home, I feel sad.

Hardly a day passes that there are not some of the Cleendra people standing or kneeling on the brae, watching across the Atlantic. Some of the older ones wondering why they cannot see their sons, daughter, brothers or sisters in that land across the ocean, as there are no hills, mounds, forests or bushes between Cleendra and America. Oh! if the naked eye could travel three thousand miles wouldn't it be a grand sight!

When I was ten years of age I was in the second book, but until I had passed into the third book I would not be looked upon as a scholar. But I could not wait. The year before had been a bad year in Scotland, and my father had not enough money home with him to pay the rent and the shop debts. It was the same with the neighbours. A crowd of us boys were got ready for the hiring fair at Strabane. Boys, oh boys, but we were glad. The big people warned us we would not have such a rush in our feet when we had the thirty-seven miles' tramp to Ballybofey past us, but we only laughed at them.

I'll always mind the morning I first left home to go to the Lagan; that was what we called the countryside beyond the mountains where boys went on hire. I think I see my mother as she handed me my four shillings for the journey. She was crying. She kissed me again and again. I can't say whether I was crying or not, though it's likely I was, for to this day it's easy to make me cry. It was in Irish she spoke and this is the sense of what she said: 'Paddy, son, here is four shillings. Two shillings will take you to the fair. If you hire, keep the other two shillings till you come home; if you don't hire, it will take you back to me. Wherever you go and wherever you be, say your prayers night and morning and say three Hail Marys to the Blessed Virgin that God will keep you from the temptations of the devil.' Everywhere you looked some mother was saying something to her own boy or girl, and I think they were all crying too. But anyway we got started. We were all barefooted; we had our boots in our bundles. There was not much weight in our bundles. There was nothing in mine, only two shirts, some patches, thread, buttons and a couple of needles.

We made a lot of noise along the road but there was still plenty of walk in us when we had finished the thirty-seven miles to Ballybofey. We lodged in a sort of barn, twenty-six boys of us on shake-downs on the floor. The old-fashioned fellows who went over the roads before advised us to take off our shirts to save ourselves from vermin. In the hurry in the morning the shirts got mixed up, but the one I got was as good as the one I lost. We paid threepence each for our night's lodging. We ate what we had left over of our pieces and started for the station. The train fare for the rest of the journey was one and twopence, so I still had one two-shilling piece, a sixpence and a penny.

When we reached Strabane we all cuddled together, and were scared at first, but the big fellows told us to scatter out so as the farmers would see us. They made us walk up and down to see how we were set up and judge what mettle was in us. Anybody who looked tired or faulty in any way was passed over. The strong boys were picked up quickly, and I was getting scared I would be left. In the end two men came to me.

'Well,' said one of them. 'Wee fellow, what wages do you want for the six months?'

I said: 'Three pounds ten.'

He said: 'Get out, you would be dear at your meat. Walk up there to the market clock until I see what you're like.'

I walked up, he followed me and made me walk back to where I started from. I heard him whispering to the other fellow: 'He is wee, but the neck is "good",'and he then offered me two pounds ten.

The other man caught both our hands in his, hit our hands a slap, and said: 'Bought and sold for three pounds.'

Wee Hughie

Elizabeth Shane

Elizabeth Shane (pseudonym of Gertrude Hind) was born in Ulster in 1877 and spent much of her life in West Donegal where her father was rector. She wrote several books of poems set in the Rosses and Gweedore. She died in County Down in 1951.

He's gone to school, Wee Hughie,
An' him not four,
Sure I saw the fright was in him
When he left the door.

But he took a hand of Denny
An' a hand of Dan,
Wi' Joe's owld coat upon him –
Och, the poor wee man!

He cut the quarest figure,
More stout nor thin,
And trottin' right an' steady,
Wi' his toes turned in.

I watched him to the corner
O' the big turf stack,
An' the more his feet went forrit,
Still his head turned back.

He was lookin', would I call him,
Och, me heart was woe –
Sure it's lost I am without him,
But he be to go.

I followed to the turnin';
When he passed it by,
God help him, he was cryin'
And maybe so was I.

The Gartan Mother's Lullaby
Joseph Campbell

Joseph Campbell (aka Seosamh Mac Cathmhaoil) was born in Belfast in 1879.
He is remembered mainly as the author of song lyrics like this. He died in
Glencree in 1944.

Sleep, O babe, for the red bee hums
The silent twilight's fall.
Aoibheall from the Grey Rock comes
To wrap the world in thrall.
A leanbhán ó, my child, my joy,
My love and heart's desire;
The crickets sing you lullaby,
Beside the dying fire.

Dusk is drawn, and the Green Man's thorn
Is wreathed in rings of joy;
Síobhra sails his boats till morn
Upon the starry bog.

A leanbhán ó, the paly moon,
Hath brimm'd her cusp in dew
And weeps to hear the sad sleep tune
I sing, O love to you.

Lough Foyle
From *A House of Children*
Joyce Cary

Joyce Cary was born in Derry in 1888 but spent much of his youth in Castlecary about seventeen miles from the city. He was many years in Africa and became well known as a novelist. He died in Oxford in 1957. In this excerpt 'Annish' is Inishowen, 'Oldcross' Carndonagh and 'Dunvil' Moville.

There is no more beautiful view in the world than that great lough, seventy square miles of salt water, from the mountains of Annish. We had heard my father call it beautiful, and so we enjoyed it with our minds as well as our feelings; keenly with both together. Wherever we went in Annish we were among the mountains and saw the lough or the ocean; often, from some high place, the whole Annish peninsula, between the two great loughs; and the Atlantic, high up in the sky, seeming like a mountain of water higher than the tallest of land. So that my memories are full of enormous skies, as bright as water, in which clouds sailed bigger than any others; fleets of monsters moving in one vast school up from the horizon and over my head, a million miles up, as it seemed to me, and then down again over the far-off mountains of Derry. They seemed to follow a curving surface of air concentric with the curve of the Atlantic which I could see bending down on either hand, a bow, which, even as a child of three or four, I knew to be the actual shape of the earth. Some grown-up, perhaps my father, had printed that upon my imagination, so that even while I was playing some childish game in the heather, red Indians or Eskimos, if I caught sight of the ocean with the tail of my eye, I would feel suddenly the roundness and independence of the world beneath me. I would feel it like a ship under my feet moving through the air just like a larger stiffer cloud, and this gave me an extraordinary exhilaration. It was expressed, of course, only in a shout or perhaps a quarrel; but it was a constant source of pleasure. I can remember jumping on a piece of hard ground, as one jumps on a deck, to test its spring, or simply to enjoy the feel of a buoyant ship beneath me.

In Annish we lived in a world which we realised as a floating planet, and in a beauty which we had been taught to appreciate, as greatly as small children are capable of enjoying spectacle. I at least enjoyed it by deliberate vision, for its sunrises and sunsets remain with me as pictures as well as a sense of glory and magnificence. I remember very well the aspect of the lough from the Oldcross road into Dunvil, a road over which I must have passed hundreds of times, especially in the spring or summer evenings. From above, the great lough, lying among its ring of mountains, would seem in the evening light like a long, low hill of water, following a different curve from the Atlantic beyond. This was because the sun, setting behind us, would cast its last greenish light on this side of the lough and leave the far side in a shadow, except where, if the wind was westerly, a silver line marked the surf. At this time, just before sunset, the sky would be full of a green radiance, fading gradually over the Derry mountains towards Belfast, into a dark blue-green transparency. As the car twisted in the winding road, we would come round to see the clouds behind us, like jagged coals in a grate, each surrounded by fire. But their centres, of course, were grey instead of black, and their fiery edges were as cold and lively with little sparks as phosphorescence on water.

The air itself, which was so dark, seemed made of this dark light, limpid like that coloured water which chemists show in their windows, and through it we could clearly see, when the car brought us round again, the iron piles of the Redman light, sometimes even the chimneys of Crowcliff on one side and Dunamara, a mile away to the south, against the livid sheen of the water.

At that time our legs could not reach to the footboard of an outside car. When it dipped outwards on a steep corner, our feet swung out until they seemed to hang over the gulf, and keeping tight hold of each other and the side rails, we could see Dunvil straight beneath them, like a map cut out of black paper and stuck down upon a globe of foil. Even the separate boats in the harbour, as small as water beetles, could be seen at their moorings, or clustered round the pier like new-hatched beetles caught in the bubbles round a willow leaf.

Bella
From *My Cousin Justin*
Margaret Barrington

Margaret Barrington was born in Malin in 1896 and was married to Edmund
Curtis and Liam O'Flaherty. She wrote many fine short stories and the novel
My Cousin Justin which is set mainly in her native village. She died in 1982.

Indoors Bella was absolute monarch. A stout woman, dressed
in the tight peasant bodice and a multitude of petticoats, over
which she tied a stiffly starched apron, she wielded her potstick
as Marshal Ney wielded his baton. Justin and I used to delight
in teasing her by picking up her skirts from behind and slipping
underneath. She would utter an unexpectedly feminine scream
and whip round with that agility which is often so surprising in
fat women.

'Take that, you young rip,' she would shout as she brought
the potstick down on the buttocks of the offender with the
precision of a drummer.

No one ever entered the kitchen without receiving either a
warning or a reprimand. No sooner was your hand on the latch
than her voice boomed out:

'Mind and wipe your feet on the mat. I won't have ye
sheddin' yer clabber all over my clean kitchen.'

Her conversation was shrewd and racy. She could curse fluently,
so she boasted, in four languages – in the English, the Gaelic of
Donegal, the Gaelic of Rachery, and the Gaelic of the Isles.

On the occasions when Wattie, as she put it, 'made a holy show
of himself", Bella always took him in hand. If he were past reason
or scorn, she would hoist him on the broad of her back like a sack

of oats and bear him out to the stables where she bedded him in the straw and left him until such time as he sobered up. On re-entering the kitchen she would wash her hands with a Pilate-like gesture and smooth her black hair behind her ears with her damp palms. Then, patting herself all over, she would remark to Theresa who sat warming her shins at the fire:

'What can ye expect from a pig but a grunt.'

She treated Wattie with the contempt she felt for all men, pouring forth her scorn at every opportunity and accusing him of all manner of misdemeanours. He paid no more heed to her nagging than a duck does to water. He accepted the position of unofficial husband with equanimity. Every Saturday morning she would rout him out of bed at five o'clock to whitewash the kitchen. When he had finished she would stand looking at it and remark:

'Lord of Creation! Isn't it a queer thing but no man alive can do anything without making a dirt? Look at the floor, will ye? By rights I should make ye go down on your marrow bones and scrub it. Heth! Since ever the curse of Adam fell on us, a man's no more use than a bull calf. What he does he has til be driven to, and when that's done, a woman must needs run after him reddin' up.'

The only man to whom she rendered lip-service was grandfather. Sometimes he would ask her into his sitting-room, give her a glass of wine and ask her to sing some old Irish song while he accompanied her on the flute. Coming as he did from the Lagan, he would discover in her singing some strange phrase he had not hitherto heard. Seated on a stiff-backed chair, her skirts outspread, her hands folded on her lap, she sang the traditional melodies with an ever-fresh abandon. Then to please grandfather she would end by singing 'The Lark in the Clear Air' in a voice as true and clear as that of the lark itself.

SAINTS AND SCHOLARS

Dies Irae
From *Altus Prosator*
Colmcille

St Colmcille was born Gartan in 521, a member of the noble Cenél Conaill. He led the mission to christianise Scotland and died in Iona, his own monastery in 597. Of the many poems attributed to his pen *Altus Prosator* is the most likely to have been written by him.

Regis regum rectissimi
prope est dies domini
dies irae et vindictae,
tenebrarum et nebulae,
diesque mirabilium
tonitruorum fortium,
dies quoque angustiae,
maeororis ac tristitiae,
in quo cessabit mulierum
amor et desiderium,
hominum que contentio
mundi huius et cupido.

Day of Wrath
From *Great Progenitor*

The day of the lord, the king most just of all kings, is near; the day of wrath and retribution; the day of darkness and clouds, of wondrous mighty thunder; a day, too, of inescapable grief and sorrow. The love and desire for women will cease and the battles of men. Love of this world will pass.

Mors Columbae
From *Vita Columbae*
Adamnán

Adamnán was born in Donegal c.628 and became ninth abbot of Iona in 679 where he wrote his life of the founder. He died there in 704.

Sed et ipse venerabilis pater in quantum poterat simul suam movebat manum; ut videlicet quod voce in egresu non valebat animae etiam motu manus fratres videretur benedicere. Et post sanctam benedictionem taliter significatam continuo spiritum exalavit.

Quo tabernaculum corporis egreso facies rubens et mirum in modum angelica visione exhilarita in tantum remansit, ut non quasi mortui sed dormientis videretur viventis. Tota interim personabat mestis plangoribus eclesia. Sed non praetereundum videtur quod eadem hora beatae transitus animae cuidam everniensi sancto revelatum est.

In illo namque monasterio quod scotica nominatur lingua Cloni-finchoil quidem homo erat sanctus senex, Christi miles, qui Lugudius vocitabatur, filius Tailchani, justus et sapiens. Hic itaque primo mane quidam eque christiano militi, Fergnovo nomine, suam enarravit visionem cum ingenti gemitu dicens: 'Hac praeterita nocte media sanctus Columba multarum columna eclesarium ad dominum transit. Et in hora beati exitus ejus Iovam insulam, ad quam corpore numquam perveni, totam angelorum claritudine in spiritu vidi inradiatam, totaque spatia aeris, usque ad ethera caelorum, eorundem angelorum claritate inlustrata, qui ad sanctam ipsius animam praeferendam de caelis misi discenderant innumeri. Altisona quoque carminalia et valde suavia audivi angelicorum coetuum cantica, eodem momento egresionis inter angelicos sanctae ipsius animae ascendentes choros'.

———

Eadem quoque hora aliam visionem aliter revelatam unus ex eis qui viderant, Christi miles, valde senex, cujus nomen etiam potest dici 'ferreolus', scotice vero Ernene, gente mocu Fir-roide, qui inter aliarum sancti Columbae monacorum reliquias, et ipse sanctus monacus, in dorso Tómme sepultus cum sanctis resurrectionem exspectat, mihi Adomnano illo juveni in tempore cum grandi retulerat testificatione, dicens: 'Illa in nocte qua sanctus Columba de terris ad caelos felici et beato fine transiit, ego et alii mecum viri laborantes in captura piscium in valle piciosi fluminis Fendae subito totum aerei inlustratum caeli spatium videmus. Cujus miraculi subitatione permoti oculus ad orientem elevatos convertimus, et ecce quasi quaedam pergrandis ignea apparuit columna, quae in illa nocte media susum ascendens ita nobis videbatur mundum inlustrare totum sicuti aesteus et meridianus sol. Et postquam illa penetravit columna caelum, quasi post occassum solis tenebrae succedunt. Hujus itaque claritundinem luminosae et praedicabilis columnae non tantum nos qui simul in eodem loco ineramus cum ingenti ammiratione vidimus, sed et alii multi piscatores qui sparsim per diversas fluminales piscinas ejusdem fluminis piscabantur, sicut nobis post retulerant, simili apparatione visa magno pavore perculsi'.

The Death of Columba
From *The Life of Columba*

And at the same time the venerable father, in so far as he could, moved his hand, so that he might be seen to bless the brothers by the motion of the hand which at the departing of his spirit he could not do by voice. And after this sacred blessing, so managed, he breathed out his life.

When he had left the tabernacle of his body his countenance continued to hold the appearance of health and, made greatly happy by the marvellous vision of angels, seemed not to be the face of a corpse but of someone alive and sleeping. Meanwhile the whole church echoed with sorrowful laments.

It seems appropriate not to omit what was revealed to a certain Irish saint at the very hour of the departure of the blessed soul. For in the monastery that in Irish is called Clonifinchoil there was an old and holy man, a soldier of Christ, sage

and just, by name Luguid, son of Tailchan. Early in the morning he told with much lamentation of a vision he had to a man called Virgno who was also a soldier of Christ: 'In the middle of last night the holy Columba, the pillar of many churches, crossed to the Lord. And in the hour of his blessed going I saw the island of Io, to which I have never been in the flesh, totally lit with the brightness of the angels. All the air right to the ethereal heavens was glowing with the splendour of those same angels, who sent in unnumbered hosts from heaven, had come down to carry up his holy soul. I heard, too, the songs of the bands of angels echoing on high and most sweet, at the instant his soul went forth among the angelic companies as they rose.

————

Another vision which occurred at the same hour was told with great insistence to me, Adamnán, then a young man, by one of those who had seen it. He was a very old soldier of Christ, whose name might be rendered 'iron man'. He was of the family mocu Fir-roide, and called in Irish Ernene. Himself a monk, he is buried with the other monks of holy Columba and awaits the resurrection with the saints in the ridge of Tóimm. He said, 'On that night when St Columba crossed from earth to heaven in a happy and holy death, I and others who were fishing in the rich vale of the river Finn suddenly noticed that the whole of the broad heaven was brightened. Disturbed by this wonder we turned our eyes to the east. And behold there had appeared in the sky what looked like a massively tall pillar which rising as it did in the middle of the night seemed to us to illuminate the whole earth like the noonday summer sun. When this pillar had pierced the heavens darkness, as after a summer sunset, returned. The brilliance of this luminous and wondrous obelisk was seen with great amazement not only by us who were together in that place but many other fishermen who were at

work at different pools of the same river were, as they told us later, stricken with great fear at seeing a like vision.

Columcille the Scribe

Anonymous

Translated by Kuno Meyer

My hand is weary with writing,
My sharp quill is not steady.
My slender beaked pen pours forth
A black draught of shining dark-blue ink.

A stream of the wisdom of blessed God
Springs from my fair brown shapely hand:
On the page it squirts its draught
Of ink of the green-skinned holly.

My little dripping pen travels
Across the plain of shining books,
Without ceasing for the wealth of the great –
Whence my hand is weary with writing.

Hard Stations
From *The Lough Derg Pilgrim*
William Carleton

William Carleton was born in Prillisk in the Clogher valley of Co Tyrone in 1794. He learnt many old stories from his father and was in his sketches and novels the first authentic recorder of the life of the nineteenth-century Irish peasant. He died in Dublin in 1869.

The first thing I did was to hand over my three cakes of oaten bread which I had got made in Petigo, tied up in a handkerchief, as well as my hat and second shirt, to the care of the owner of one of the huts: having first, by the way, undergone a second prostration on touching the island, and greeted it with fifteen holy kisses, and another string of prayers. I then, according to the regulations, should commence the *stations*, lacerated as my feet were after so long a journey; so that I had not a moment to rest. Think, therefore, what I must have suffered, on surrounding a large chapel, in the direction of from east to west, over a pavement of stone spikes, every one of them making its way along my nerves and muscles to my unfortunate brain. I was absolutely stupid and dizzy with the pain, the praying, the jostling, the elbowing, the scrambling and the uncomfortable penitential murmurs of the whole crowd. I knew not what I was about, but went through the forms in the same mechanical spirit which pervaded all present. As for that solemn, humble, and heartfelt sense of God's presence, which Christian prayer demands, its existence in the mind would not only be a moral but a physical impossible in Lough Dearg. I verily think that if mortification of the body, without conversion of the life and heart – if penance and not repentance *could* save the soul, no wretch who performed a pilgrimage here could with a good grace be damned. Out of hell the place is matchless, and if there *be* a purgatory in the other world, it may very well be said there is a fair rehearsal of it in the county of Donegal in Ireland.

When I commenced my station, I started from what is called the 'Beds', and God help St Patrick if he lay upon them: they are sharp stones placed circularly in the earth, with the spike ends of them up, one circle within another; and the manner in which the pilgrim gets as far as the innermost, resembles precisely that in which school-boys enter the 'Walls of Troy' upon their slates. I moved away from these upon the sharp stones with which the whole island is surfaced, keeping the chapel, or 'Prison', as it is called, upon my right; then turning, I came round again, with a *circumbendibus*, to the spot from which I set out. During the circuit, as well as I can remember, I *repeated* fifty-five *paters* and *aves*, and five creeds, or five decades; and be it known that the fifty prayers were offered up to the Virgin Mary, and the odd five to God! I then commenced getting round the external beds, during which I *repeated*, I think, fifteen *paters* and *aves* more; and as the beds decreased in circumference, the prayers decreased in length, until a short circuit and three *paters* and *aves* finished the last and innermost of these blessed couches. I really forget how many times each day the prison and these beds are to be surrounded, and how many hundred prayers are to be *repeated* during the circuit, though each circuit is in fact making the grand tour of the island; but I shall never forget that I was the best part of a July day at it, when the soles of my feet were flayed, and the stones hot enough to broil a beefsteak! When the first day's station was over, is it necessary to say that a little rest would have been agreeable? But no, this would not suit the policy of the place:

here it may be truly said that there is no rest for the wicked. The only luxury allowed me was the privilege of feasting upon one of my cakes (having not tasted food that blessed day until then); upon one of my cakes, I say, and a copious supply of the water of the lake, which, to render the repast more agreeable, was rendered lukewarm! This was to keep my spirits up after the delicate day's labour I had gone through, and to cheer me against the pleasant prospect of a hard night's praying without sleep, which lay in the back ground!

Father O'Flynn

A. P. Graves

Arthur Percival Graves was born in Dublin in 1884, the son of a clergyman who afterwards became Bishop of Limerick. He was on the staff of *Punch* and later became a school inspector. A compiler of many anthologies of Irish poetry he is now best known as the father of the poet and novelist, Robert Graves. He died in Wales in 1931.

Of priests we can offer a charmin' variety,
Far renowned for larnin' and piety;
Still, I'd advance you, widout impropriety,
    Father O'Flynn as the flower of them all.

Chorus
Here's a health to you, Father O'Flynn,
Slainte, and slainte, and slainte agin'
    Powerfulest preacher, and
    Tinderest teacher, and
Kindliest creature in ould Donegal.

Don't talk of your Provost and Fellows of Trinity,
Famous for ever at Greek and Latinity
Dad and the divels and all at Divinity,
    Father O'Flynn'd make hares of them all.
        Come, I vinture to give you my word,
        Never the likes of his logic was heard
            Down from Mythology
            Into Thayology.
        Troth, and Conchology, if he'd the call.
Chorus

Och, Father O'Flynn, you've the wonderful way wid you
All ould sinners are wishful to pray wid you,
All the young childer are wild for to play wid you,
    You've such a way wid you, Father avick,
Still, for all you've so gentle a soul,
        Gad, you've your flock in the grandest conthroul:
            Checking the crazy ones,
            Coaxin' onaisy ones,
        Liftin' the lazy ones on wid the stick.
Chorus

And though quite avoidin' all foolish frivolity
Still at all seasons of innocent jollity,
Where was the play-boy could claim an equality
    At comicality, Father, wid you?
        Once the Bishop looked grave at your jest,
        Till this remark sent him off wid the rest,
            'Is it the gaiety
            All to the laity?
        Cannot the clargy be Irishmen too?'
Chorus

Pilgrims
From *Lough Derg*
Patrick Kavanagh

Patrick Kavanagh was born in Co Monaghan in 1904 and worked as farmer
and cobbler before taking up an often turbulent career as journalist, poet
and novelist. *Lough Derg* was written in 1942 when the pilgrimage to the
penitential island was part of the Irish year. He died in Dublin in 1967.

From Cavan and from Leitrim and from Mayo,
From all the thin-faced parishes where hills
Are perished noses running peaty water,
They come to Lough Derg to fast and pray and beg
With all the bitterness of nonentities, and the envy
Of the inarticulate when dealing with the artist.
Their hands push closed the doors that God holds open;
Love-sunlit is an enchanter in June's hours
And flowers and light. These to shopkeepers and small
    lawyers
Are heresies up beauty's sleeve.
The naïve and simple go on pilgrimage too,
Lovers trying to take God's truth for granted . . .
Listen to the chanted
Evening devotions in the limestone church,
For this is Lough Derg, St Patrick's Purgatory.
He came to this island-acre of limestone once
To be shut of the smug too-faithful. The story
Is different now.
Solicitors praying for cushy jobs
To be County Registrar or Coroner,

Shopkeepers threatened with sharper rivals
Than any hook-nosed foreigner.
Mothers whose daughters are Final Medicals,
Too heavy-hipped for thinking,
Wives whose husbands have angina pectoris,
Wives whose husbands have taken to drinking.

But there were the sincere as well
The innocent who feared the hell
Of sin. The girl who had won
A lover and the girl who had none
Were both in trouble
Trying to encave in the rubble
Of these rocks the Real,
The part that can feel.
And the half-pilgrims too,
They who are the true
Spirit of Ireland, who joke
Through the Death-mask and take
Virgins of heaven or flesh,
Were on Lough Derg Island
Wanting some half-wish.

LABHRAÍTEAR GAEILGE ANSEO

Sean-Dún na nGall

Ní fios cé ahum

A poem dating from the turn of the century and ascribed to a woman teacher from Rathmullan perhaps called O'Boyce.

Is grá geal mo chroí thú, 'Thír Chonaill, a stór,
'Do luí mar bheadh seoid ghlas san fharraige mhór;
Ó gráim thú i gconaí go moch is go mall
'S molfaidh mé a choích' thú, a shean-Dún na nGall.

Níl contae i nÉirinn níos deise ná thú,
Níl daoine sa domhan mhór níos fearr cáil is clú
Ná tá i dTír Chonaill abhus agus thall,
Ó! Bláth bán ár dtíre thú, a shean-Dún na nGall.

Tá teanga ár sinsir da labhairt ann go fóill
Chomh milis bin blasta le hamhrán nó ceol
Na n-aingeal sna Flaithis gan smachtú gan smál,
Ó gráim go deo thú, a shean-Dún na nGall.

Old Donegal

You're the bright love of my heart, Tír Chonaill, my treasure,
Lying like a green gem in the ocean;
I love you early and late
And will praise you for ever, old Donegal.

No county in Ireland is more beautiful than you;
No earthly people own greater respect
Than those in Tír Chonaill wherever you look,
O! You're the flower of our country, old Donegal.

The language of our forefathers is still spoken there
As sweet and as tuneful as the music made
By the free spotless angels in paradise;
O, I will love you eternally, old Donegal.

Báidín Fheilimí

Ní fios cé a chum

Popular children's song from northwest Donegal

Báidín Fheilimí d'imigh go Gabhla
Báidín Fheilimí 's Feilimí ann.
  (faoi dhó)

Curfá:
Báidín bídeach, báidín beosach,
Báidín bóidheach, báidín Fheilimí;
Báidín díreach, báidín deontach
Báidín Fheilimí 's Feilimí ann.

Báidín Fheilimí d'imigh go Toraigh
Báidín Fheilimí 's Feilimí ann.
  (faoi dhó)
Curfá

Báidín Fheilimí briseadh i dToraigh í
Báidín Fheilimí 's Feilimí ann.
  (faoi dhó)
Curfá

Feilimi's Little Boat

Feilimi's little boat went to Gola
Feilimí's boat with Feilimí inside.
            (twice)

Chorus
A tiny boat, a lively boat,
A bonny boat, Feilimí's boat;
A trusty boat, a steerable boat
Feilimí's boat with Feilimí inside.

Feilimí's little boat went to Tory
Feilimí's boat with Feilimí inside.
            (twice)
Chorus

Feilimí's boat was broken at Tory
Feilimí's boat with Feilimi inside.
            (twice)
Chorus

Seacht gCineál Meisce
As 'An Chéad Meisce agus an Meisce Dheireanach'
Seán Bán Mac Meanman

Seán Bán MacMeanman was born in Kingarrow near Fintown in 1891 and taught Irish in Glenties, once losing his position for refusing to swear an oath of allegiance to the state. This excerpt comes from his book *Fear Siúil* (1924). He died in 1961.

. . . Ag dul suas an baile sin domh casadh duine aitheantais orm, fear as an áit a dtuga siad Mícheál Beag Ó Connacháin air. Chuir sé forrán orm agus stop mé.

'Is é do bheatha ar ais,' arsa seisean.

'Go raibh maith agat,' arse mise.

'Fuair tú iomlán na fearthainne,' arsa seisean.

'Tá mé go díreach mar a tharraingeofaí amach as an abhainn mé,' arsa mé féin.

Ní dhearna Mícheál dada ach greim gualann a fháil orm is mé a streachailt isteach go tigh leanna a bhí ar ár ngaobhair. Thug sé cogar don fhear a bhí i gcúl an chuntair is cuireadh dhá ghloine anall.

'Anois, ól sin,' arsa Mícheál, ag tabhairt ceann de na gloiní domh.

'Cad é atá ann?' arsa mise.

'Tá sláinte agus íochsláinte ann,' arsa Mícheál, 'is ba chóir nach mbeadh méar a dhíth ar an té a gcaithfear an fhearthainn a fháscadh amach as a léinidh anocht.'

Chuir mé an gloine le mo phuisíní.

'A Athair Shíoraí!' arsa mise, 'biotáilte atá ann agus an pledge ormsa.'

'Seo, seo, caith siar é is ná bí ag glagaireacht fá phledge,' arsa Mícheál. 'Tá an pledge ort anocht is beidh an slaghdán ort ar maidin amárach' arsa seisean, 'is bíodh a fhios agat nach mbíonn mórán truaighe duit ansin. Agus má ghlacann tú pliúraisi nó an chréacht, deárfaidh go leor: "Bhí sé amuigh lá na fearthainne móire go raibh sé báite ach ní ligfeadh an righneas dó dada a ghlacadh a theífeadh é, is nár fhóire air! nó is beag an scéal anois é."'

D'éist mé le caint Mhícheáil; bhí a fhios agam go raibh sé ag inse na fírinne, is cha raibh mé riamh dochomhairleach. Níor dhúirt mé focal ach thóg mé an gloine is bhain mé bolgam as. Bhí bruith-theas ann agus, ainneoin go raibh an blas maith agus fíormhaith, b'éigean domh cár a chur orm féin nó shíl mé go raibh mo theanga is mo scornach scallta.

'Seo do shláinte!' arsa Mícheál, is d'fholmhaigh sé a ghloine féin – ní raibh méar ar bith a dhíth air.

'Sláinte agus saol duit!' arsa mise, agus chuir mé an gloine ar mo cheann is níor fhág me deoir ann. Ansin d'ordaigh mise an traet céanna arís. Fuair muid sin is d'ól muid é in am gairid. Cé a thainig isteach ansin ach fear aitheantais eile, fear de thógáil na háite. Bhuail seisean an bord is scairt na traetanna céanna arís. Níor chuir Mícheál suas dó is ní thiocfadh liomsa a bheith corr. hÓladh an tríú traet is lig mise síos an tríú gloine den digh chéanna. Dúirt mé féin ansin go raibh an t-am imeacht agus amach linn uilig. Ach cé a casadh orainn ag maide an dorais ach fear an tí, an fear ar leis an teach tábhairne . . .

———

Bhog mé liom. Deirtí roimhe seo go raibh seacht gcineál meisce ann: meisce chaointe, meisce bhrúine, meisce chrábhaidh, meisce gháirí, meisce stangaireachta, meisce bhreallánachta agus meisce chodlata. Cé acu atá nó nach bhfuil, ní dheachaigh mise i bhfad gur bhuail tallann úrnua mé: tharraing mé amach mo phaidrín, chuaigh mé thar na chúig deichniúir dhéag is cluinfeá mé leathmhíle ar shiúl. Agus ní hé amháin sin ach bhí oiread rioball agam ar an phaidrín is a bhí ag Éamonn Mhícheáil Mhóir ar aon phaidrín dá dtug sé amach riamh i dtigh faire. Cha raibh mé riamh comh cráifeach roimhe sin nó ó shin. Dá bhfaighinn bás san am sílim go rachainn suas chun na bhFlaitheas idir chorp is chleiteacha. Nuair a stad mé a dh'urnaí, bhuail taom caointe mé is thoisigh mé is ghoil mé mo sháith.

Ní thiocfaidh liom insin anois cad é a rinne mé nó cad é nach ndearna mé ina ndhiaidh sin. Ní thiocfaidh liom a insin lá arna mhárach. Ach tá cineál marbhcuimhne agam nach raibh sé i bhfad ina ndiaidh sin go raibh mé i mo shuí ag an tinidh i dtigh mo loistín, cailín ar mo chul is greim cinn aici orm agus cailín eile ag cur tae ionam le spanóig. Caithfidh sé gur chaill mé iomlán mo mhothaithe is gur thit mé thart i ndiaidh an tae.

———

Sin chugaibh anois cuntas beacht ar an chéad mheisce agus an mheisce dheireanach a chuir mé tharam. Tá sin daichead bliain ag Féile Mhíchil seo chuaigh thart agus níor bhlais mé aon deoir ó shin.

———

Translation

Seven Kinds of Drunkenness

———

As I made my way through the village I met an acquaintance, a man from the place called Michael Beag Conaghan. He hailed me and made me stop.

'You're welcome back,' said he.

'Thanks,' said I.

'You got all that rain,' said he.

'You'd think I'd just been pulled out of the river,' I said.

Michael caught me by the shoulder and hustled me into a pub nearby. He whispered to the man behind the counter and two glasses were pushed over.

'Now drink that down!' said Michael, handing one to me.

'What's in it?' I asked.

'There's health and healing in it,' said Michael, 'and no man who has to wring the rain out of his shirt tonight should need to be coaxed.'

I put the glass to my lips.

'Good God,' I gasped, 'there's alcohol in it and me with the pledge.'

'Come on! Toss it back there and stop your gabbling about a pledge,' said Michael. 'You have the pledge tonight and you'll have a cold tomorrow; and you may as well know that nobody will have any sympathy for you. And if you get pleurisy or consumption, most people will say: "He was out that day that the rain was so heavy and he got soaked. But he was too stubborn to take anything to warm him and he deserves nothing better."

I listened to what Michael said. I knew that he was telling the truth and I was never hard to persuade. I said nothing, put the glass to my lips and took a sip. It was burning hot and although the flavour was good, indeed, very good, I could not help making a face. I thought my tongue and my throat were scalded.

'Your good health,' said Michael and emptied his own glass; he did not need any coaxing!

'Health and long life to you!' I said and putting the glass to my head I drank it every drop. Then I ordered another round of the same. It arrived and we downed it quickly. Who should come in then but another pal who was from the district. He rapped the bar and called for the same again. Michael did not object and I couldn't be odd. The third treat was drunk: I lowered a third glass of the same drink. I announced that it was time to go and out we all went. But who should we meet at the lintel but the host, the owner of the pub . . .

———

I moved on. It has been said that there are seven kinds of drunkenness: lachrymose, sorrowful, pious, giggling, argumentative, foolish and sleepy. Whatever about that I hadn't gone very far when a fit of praying hit me. I pulled out my beads and went right through the fifteen decades. You could have heard me half a mile away. Not only that but I had as many trimmin's as Eamonn Michael Mór ever had giving out the rosary at a wake. I have never been so pious before or since. If I had died then I think I would have gone straight to heaven. When I was finished praying a paroxysm of weeping seized me and I cried my heart out.

I can't say what I may have done after that but I have a notion that it was not much later that I found myself sitting by the fire in my digs, with one of the maids holding my head and the other spooning tea into me. I must have lost all sensation and dropped off after the tea . . .

———

Well that was my first and last bender. It happened forty years ago last Michaelmas and I haven't touched a drop since.

Séimí Phádraig Duibh
From *Caisleáin Óir*
'*Máire*'

Séamus Ó Grianna was born in Ranafast in 1891 and was a schoolteacher, an anti-Treatyite and a civil servant working mainly for *An Gúm*. He wrote several novels including *Mo Dhá Róisín* and *Caisleáin Óir*, taking his mother's forename as *nom-de-plume*, but is best known for his many books of short stories. He died in Dublin in 1969.

Bhí scaifte gasúr, agus Séimí ina measc, bhí sin ina seasamh ina rang thíos i gceann an tí agus gasúr den chuid ba mhó in ainm a bheith á dteagasc. Ach chonaic an Rí an teagasc sin: ag imirt chnaipí, ag déanamh malairteach, agus ag caitheamh seileog ar a chéile.

I gceann tamaill tharraing an máistir air an leabhar mór agus thoisigh sé a scairteadh amach ainmneach. Scairt sé ceann amháin trí huaire, agus a ghlór ag airdiú 'ach aon uair, ach ní thug duine ar bith freagra air. Bhí na páistí uilig agus a súile sáite i Séimí acu, agus iontas an domhain ar Shéimí bhocht goidé a bhí ar cois. Sa deireadh anuas leis an mháistir go ceann an tí agus slat saileoige leis ina láimh. Thóg sé an tslat os cionn Shéimí agus thug a chorp don fhear a bhí thíos, goidé a thug air gan freagra a thabhairt ar a ainm. D'amharc an leanbh suas air agus cigilt ina mhuineál le heagla roimh na buillí.

'Labhair, marbhfáisc ort, labhair, a smuilcín gan mhúineadh. Cád chuige nach dtug tú freagra ar d'ainm?' arsa an máistir.

'Níor chuala mé thú,' arsa an leanbh, agus glór an chaointe ina cheann.

'Cluin sin,' arsa an máistir, ag tarraingt na slaite aniar fríd an chloiginn air. Agus tharraing sé an dara leadhb sna cluasa air agus an triú ceann sa chaoldroim.

'A mhaistín cháidhigh na mbréag, i ndiaidh mé "James Gallagher" a scairteadh trí huaire seanard mo chinn, a rá is de go n-abair tú nár chuala tú mé. Is maith an rud a dhéanfas tú nuair a thiocfas ann duit, nuair a fuair tú de chroí bréagach a thabhairt domhsa an chéad lá in Éirinn.'

'Shíl mise,' arsa an leanbh, agus dhá chuid á dhéanamh den fhocal ina bhéal leis an smeacharnaigh, 'shíl mé nach James Gallagher a bhí orm ach Séimí Phádraig Duibh.'

Fágadh iomlán na bpáistí sioctha leis na gáirí. Rinne an máistir é féin draothadh beag tirim drochmheasúil.

'Bíodh a fhios agat nach Séimí Phádraig Dhuibh d'ainm níos faide,' ar seisean. 'Ar scor ar bith ní hé d'ainm i dteach na scoile é. Thig leat do rogha ainm a bheith ort nuair atá tú ag gabháil thart fán ghríosaigh sa bhaile ag glúine do mháthartha móire. Ach ní bheidh Séimí Phádraig Duibh nó Séimí ar bith eile anseo ort. Bíodh a fhios agat nach i seanchró d'athara atá tú anois, ach i scoil na banríona. Bíodh a fhios agat an méid sin, a uascáin cháidhigh na mbratóg.

Translation

Séimí Phádraig Duibh

A group of boys with Séimí in their midst were standing down at one end of the building with a senior boy supposedly teaching them. But heaven help the teaching: they were playing with buttons, swapping and spitting at each other.

After a while the master pulled the big book to him and began calling out names. One he called three times, his voice rising each time, but no one responded. All the children fixed their eyes on Séimí and the poor fellow had no idea what on earth was wrong. Eventually up came the master to the end of the room carrying a salley rod in his hand. He raised the rod above Séimí's head and asked him why the devil he hadn't answered to his name. The child gazed up at him, his chin trembling at the thought of being hit.

'Speak, curse you, you unmannerly brat! Why didn't you answer your name?' said the master.

'I didn't hear you,' said the child, half crying.

'Then hear this!' said the master, bringing the rod down on his head. He hit him a second blow about the ears and a third in the small of his back.

'You filthy lying cur to say, that after me calling "James Gallagher" three times at the top of my voice, you didn't hear me! You'll be a right criminal when you come of age if you can be such a liar at the start.'

'I thought,' said the child, his speech broken with sobbing, that my name was Séimí Phádraig Duibh, not James Gallagher.'

The whole school was transfixed with laughter. Even the master managed a malevolent little dry smile.

'Get it into your head that Séimí Phádraig Duibh isn't your name any more,' he said. 'At any rate it'll not be your name at school. You can have any name you like when you are scrabbling in the ashes at home about your Granny's knee. But you'll not be Séimí Phádraig Duibh or Séimí anything else here. You'd better realise that you're not in your father's oul' hut now but in the Queen's school. Understand that you dirty raggedy brat!'

TRÁTHNÓNA BEAG ARÉIR

'Máire'

Thíos i lár a' ghleanna, tráthnóna beag aréir,
Agus an drúcht 'na deora geala 'na luí ar bharr an fhéir,
Sea casadh domhs' an ainnir ab áille gnúis is pearsa,
Is í a sheol mo stuaim 'un seachráin tráthnóna beag aréir.
Cúrfa:
Agus a Rí nár lách ár n-ealaín dul síos a' gleann aréir,
Ag éalú fríd a' chanach agus ciúnas ann sa spéir.
Ó, a rún mo chléibh nár mhilis ár súgradh croí nár ghairid
Is a Rí na glóire gile tabhair ar ais an oích' aréir.

II

Do chiabhfolt fáinneach frasach, do mhalaidh bhán 's do dhéad,
Do chaolchoim álainn mhaiseach, is glórthaí caoin' do bhéil,
Do bhráid mar chlúmh na heala, do shúil mar réalt na mara,
'S faraor gur dhual dúinn scaradh tráthnóna beag aréir.

III

Dá bhfaighinnse 'rís cead pilleadh agus labhairt le stór mo
    cléibh,
Nó dá bhfaighinnse buaidh ar chinniúint chár mhiste liom
    fán saol.
Shiúlfainn leat fríd chanach 's fríd mhéilt' ar chiumhais na
    mara
Agus Dúthaigh Dé dá gcaillfinn go bpógfainnse do bhéal.

Late Yesterday Evening

Down in the middle of the glen, late yesterday evening,
When the dew hung in bright drops on the tips of the grass,
I chanced upon a maiden, beautiful in face and form;
And she drove my brain distracted, late yesterday evening.

Great God, was not our time all pleasant going down the glen
    last night
As we stole through the bog white with cotton under a quiet
    sky?
O love of my soul was not our sport delighful though sadly
    short in time!
O king of brightest glory give me last night back again.

Your hair in tumbling ringlets, your snow-white brow and teeth,
Your waist of slender beauty, and the soft sounds of your
    mouth,
Your neck as soft as swansdown, your eye like the star of the
    sea,
Alas that we had to separate late yesterday evening.

If I'm ever granted access and can speak with my love again,
If I could change my destiny I'd accept what might befall.
I would walk with you by bog blossoms and the dunes at the
    ocean's marge
I'd thrust away God's paradise and fasten on your mouth.

Jams O'Donnell
From *An Béal Bocht*
Myles na gGopaleen

Myles na gCopaleen (aka Flann O'Brien) was born Brian O'Nolan in 1911 in
Strabane (only the width of the river Mourne from Donegal). He had a
pyrotechnic career as a satirist working as columnist, novelist and playwright.
An Béal Bocht is a skit on the pluvial Donegal novels of such Gaelic writers
as Máire. He died in 1966.

Bhailíomar go léir isteach i dTigh na Scoile, cró beag mí-mhaisiúil
a raibh an fluichras ag sileadh anuas ar na ballaí, agus gach ní
bog tais ann. Shuíomar uilig ar bhinsi gan focal gan bíog asainn
ar eagla an mháistir. Chaith sé a shúla nimhneacha ar folúin ar
fud an tighe gur thuirlingid ormsa agus gur fhan orm. Dar fia
nár aoibhinn liom a radharc orm, an dá shúil sin dom chriathrú.
Taréis tamailín dhírigh sé méar fhada bhuí orm agus aduirt:

'*Phwat is yer nam?*'

Níor thuigeas an chaint seo ná aon chaint eile bítear ag
cleachtú ar an gcoigrích i gcéin, gan agam acht an Ghaeilg
amháin mar ghléas labhartha agus mar dhíon ar dheacractaí an
tsaoil. Níor fhéadas acht stanadh air, mé balbh ón bhfaitíos.
Chonnac annsin go raibh racht mór feirge ag teacht air agus ag
méadú de réir a chéile mar bhéadh néal fearthana ann.
Bhreathnúios thart go scaolmhar ar na macaoimh eile. Chuala
cogar ar mo chúl:

'T'ainm tá uaidh!'

Bhíog mo chroí le háthas ón bhfortacht so agus bhíos buíoch
don té bhí dom phromptáil. Dfhéachas go cneasta ar an mhaistir

agus dfhreagair é:

'Bónapáirt Mícheálangaló Pheadair Eoghain Shorcha Thomáis Mháire Sheáin Shéamais Dhiarmada . . . '

Sula raibh ráite ná leath-ráite agam tháinic tafán conafach on mháistir agus ghlaodh sé orm aníos chuige lena mhéir. An uair a thánach fad leis bhí maide ramha fálta aige 'na ghlaich. Bhí rabhartha feirge ag gabháil de fa'n am so, agus bhí greim chun gnótha aige ar an mhaide lena dhá láimh. Tharraing sé thar a ghualain é agus thug anuas orm go tréan le fead gaoithe, gur bhuail buille tubaisteach sa chloigean orm. Thuiteas i laige on mbuille sin acht sular cailleadh na céadfaithe ar fad orm chuala scread uaidh:

'*Yer nam*,' ar seisean, '*is Jams O'Donnell*.'

Jams O'Donnell? Bhí an dá bhriathar so ag gliogaireacht im cheann nuair tháinic mothú arís ann. Fuaireas mé féin sínte ar leataoibh ar an urlar, mo bhríste, mo ghruaig agus mo phearsa uile ar maothas ó na slaoda fola bhí ag stealadh ón scoilt bhí fághtha ag an mhaide ar mo chloigean. An t-am abhí neart ceart arís ins na súla agam, bhí macaomh eile ar a bhonnaí agus a ainm a fhiafrai dhe. Is léir nach raibh críonacht ar bith sa tachrán so, agus ní raibh deá-chomhairle a leasa féin bainte aige as an ngriosáil buailte a fuair mise, mar dfhreagair sé an máistir agus dúirt a ainm tuata díreach mo dhálta féin. Tharraing an maistir an maide ina ghlaic ath-uair agus níor stop go raibh fuil an mhacaoimh seo go líonmhar aige a dórtadh, an machaomh féin gan aon mhothú anois ann acht a mhalairt go fírinneach, é sínte 'na chuachán fola ar an urlár. Agus le linn an bhuailte scread an mháistir arís:

'*Yer nam is Jams O'Donnell*.'

Mar sin go dtí go raibh gach créatúr sa scoil treascairte aige agus *Jams O'Donnell* tabhartha ainm ortha go léir. Ní raibh aon cloigean óg gan scoilteadh sa dúthaigh an lá san . . .

Jams O'Donnell

Translated by Flann O'Brien

We all gathered into the schoolhouse, a small unlovely hut where the rain ran down the walls and everything was soft and damp. We all sat on benches, without a word or a sound for fear of the master. He cast his venomous eyes over the room and they alighted on me where they stopped. By jove! I did not find his look pleasant while these two eyes were sifting me. After a while he directed a long yellow finger at me and said

– Phwat is yer nam?

I did not understand what he said nor any other type of speech which is practised in foreign parts because I had only Gaelic as a mode of expression and a protection against the difficulties of life. I could only stare at him, dumb with fear. I then saw a great fit of rage come over him and gradually increase exactly like a rain-cloud. I looked around timidly at the other boys. I heard a whisper at my back:

– Your name he wants!

My heart leaped with joy at this assistance and I was grateful to him who prompted me. I looked politely at the master and replied to him:

– Bonaparte, son of Michelangelo, son of Peter, son of Owen, son of Thomas's Sarah, granddaughter of John's Mary, grand-daughter of James, son of Dermot . . .

Before I had uttered or half-uttered my name, a rabid bark issued from the master and he beckoned to me with his finger.

By the time I had reached him he had an oar in his grasp. Anger had come over him in a flood-tide at this stage and he had a businesslike grip of the oar in his two hands. He drew it over his shoulder and brought it down hard upon me with a swish of air, dealing me a destructive blow on the skull. I fainted from that blow but before I became totally unconscious I heard him scream:

– Yer nam, said he, is Jams O'Donnell!

Jams O'Donnell? These two words were singing in my ears when feeling returned to me. I found that I was lying on my side on the floor, my breeches, hair and all my person saturated with the streams of blood which flowed from the split caused by the oar in my skull. When my eyes were in operation again, there was another youngster on his feet being asked his name. It was apparent that this child lacked shrewdness completely and had not drawn good beneficial lessons for himself from the beating I had received because he replied to the master, giving his common name as I had. The master again brandished the oar which was in his grasp and did not cease until he was shedding blood plentifully, the youngster being left unconscious and stretched out on the floor, a bloodied bundle. And during the beating the master screamed once more:

– Yer nam is Jams O'Donnell!

He continued in this manner until every creature in the school had been struck down by him and all had been named *Jams O'Donnell*. No young skull in the countryside that day remained unsplit . . .

Fear Antrathach
From *Creach Choinn Uí Dhónaill*
AD 1495
Seosamh Mac Grianna

Seosamh Mac Grianna was born in Ranafast in 1901 and like his brother 'Máire' was teacher, republican and *An Gúm* translator. He produced in spite of poor health some of the finest modern writing in Irish. He died in Letterkenny in 1990.

Oíche rinneach réaltógach a raibh Conn mac Aodha Rua, mhic Néill Gairbh, mhic Tharlaigh an Fhíona Uí Dhónaill, ag caitheamh fleá agus féasta i gCaisleán Dhún na nGall, bhí fear anthrathach uaigneach ag teacht tríd an Bhearnas Mhór le coim na hóíche. Ní soiléir a bhí sé in íochtar dhuibheagán an ghleanna, an áit a raibh sé ó sholas sular chaill siad an ghrian ag Málainn Mhóir. Agus ba lúide na sin a bhí sé inchluinte, óir ba gheall le coiscéim an fhia siúl fir in Éirinn san am, agus bhí sruthán ag teacht ón tsliabh a bhí ag cur a ngáire ar fud an aeir i dtólamh mar a bheadh anáil an phíobaire ag buanú na fuaime sa phíb. Ba iad na súile an chuid de ar lú ar luigh an dorchadas orthu, mura dtrachtfaimis ar an bhiorán bhrollaigh den ór loiscthe a bhí in uachtar a bhrád. Súile lonracha a bhí iontú, a d'iompair an solas, agus bhí siad lán uabhair agus uafais an uair thostach sin, ag amharc ar na sléibhte a bhí crochta os a chionn mar a bheadh dhá bhruach bearna a bhí ag dul ó uachtar an domhain go dtí íochtar an domhain.

Bhí cúig mhíle de ghleann ina ndiaidh siar go dtí an áit a raibh loch Muirne ina luí ag fanacht le gealach agus cúig mhíle roimhe sula gcastaí áras duine air, ar ucht léana, an áit ar dual conaí agus cothú a dheanamh. Tháinig sé anoir ó Chaisleán na Finne an lá roimhe sin, agus fuair sé aíocht fhlaithiúil i dteach biataigh idir sin agus Baile Bó Féich. Agus tharla an lá seo é ag cur aithne ar shléibhte Thír Chonaill. D'éirigh siad roimhe idir an meán lae agus an nóin, fána sleasa fada gormcheocha, néalta neimhe ag sciobadh fana mbaithis mar a bheadh folt fionn fada ag scaipeadh le síon, iad gágach le srutháin agus giobach le fraoch agus garbh le scileach agus le cruachonamar creag.

Tharraing siad a n-anáil (agus duine ar bith a chonaic sléibhte Thír Chonaill tá a fhios aige go tarraingíonn siad a n-anáil), agus má bhí ocras air níor ghoin sé é, agus má bhí tuirse air níor chloígh sé é, nuair a tógadh a aigne chun machnamh ar fhairsingeach nach mbíodh sé air de gnáth, ina fhile fhíoranta agus mar a bhí sé. Níor tháinig aisling nó samhailt ghlinn faoina mheanma; ach mhothaigh sé só mór fairsing neartmhar ag folcadh na hinntinne aige; bhí sé ina chara ag an néal mhór a bhí ag seoladh ar ucht na spéire, agus ina chéile ag an ghealach a bhí ag gluaiseacht ar na mullaí dubha mar a bheadh cnag óir a bheadh idir chámáin ag na fathaigh a bhí sa thír nuair a mhair Lugh agus Gaibhide agus Balar na mBéimeann ó thuaidh.

Sinister Man
From *The Spoil of Conn O'Donnell*

One frosty starry night when Conn, son of Red Hugh, son of Rough Niall, son of Tarlach of the Wine, O'Donnell was holding a great feast in Donegal castle a sinister, solitary man made his way at nightfall through Barnesmore. He was practically invisible in the dark floor of the glen where there had been no light since the sun disappeared at Malinmore. His progress was just as silent, for men were as light of foot as deer in the Ireland of the time and the streams that gurgled down from the mountain filled the air continuously with their laughter like a piper building up sound in his pipes. The only brightness about him was to be found in his eyes, if you were to ignore the breast pin of hammered gold that held his cloak. They were glittering eyes that held the light and they were filled with pride and awe at that silent hour as they gazed at the mountains that beetled above him like the two sides of an abyss that could split the world in two.

He had put five miles behind him from the place where Lough Mourne lay waiting for the moon and another five had to be traversed until he would come upon human habitation, by the water's edge, where he could find food and shelter. He had come west from Castlefin the day before and he had been received hospitably at an inn between there and Ballybofey. Today he had been introduced to the hills of Donegal. They had risen before him between noon and evening, long sloping blue-misted terraces, with high clouds

Anseo ag Stáisiún Chaiseal na gCorr
Do Michael Davitt
Cathal Ó Searcaigh

Cathal Ó Searcaigh was born in Mín a' Leá, Gortahork, County Donegal in 1954. He is one of the leading Irish-language poets.

Anseo ag Stáisiún Chaiseal na gCorr
d'aimsigh mise m'oileán rúin
mo thearmann is mo shanctóir.
Anseo braithim i dtiúin
le mo chinniúint féin is le mo thimpeallacht.
Anseo braithim seasmhacht
is mé ag feaceáil chríocha mo chineáil
thart faoi bhun an Eargail
mar a bhfuil siad ina gcónaí go ciúin
le breis agus trí chéad bliain
ar mhínte féaraigh an tsléibhe
ó Mhín 'a Leá go Mín na Craoibhe.
Anseo, foscailte os mo chomair
go díreach mar bhéadh leabhar ann
tá an taobh tíre seo anois
ó Dhoire Chonaire go Prochlais.
Thíos agus thuas tím na gabháltais
a briseadh as béal an fhiántais.
Seo duanaire mo mhuintire;
an lámhscríbhinn a shaothraigh siad go teann
le dúch a gcuid allais.
Anseo tá achan chuibhreann mar bheadh rann ann

i mórdhán an mhíntíreachais.
Léím anois eipic seo na díograise
i gcanúint ghlas na ngahbáltas
is tuigim nach bhfuilim ach ag comhlíonadh dualgais
is mé as tabhairt dhúslán an Fholúis
go díreach mar a thug mo dhaoine dúshlán an fiántais
le dícheall agus le dúthracht
gur thuill siad an duais.
Anseo braithim go bhfuil éifeacht i bhfilíocht.
Braithim go bhfuil brí agus tábhacht liom mar dhuine
is mé ag feidhmiú mar chuisle de chroí mo chine
agus as an chinnteacht sin tagann suimhneas aigne.
Ceansaítear mo mhianta, séimhítear mo smaointe,
cealaítear contrárthachtaí ar an phointe.

Here at Caiseal na gCorr Station
Translated by Gabriel Fitzmaurice

Here at Caiseal na gCorr Station
I have discovered my hidden island,
my refuge, my sanctuary.
Here I find myself in tune
with my fate and environment.
Here I feel permanence
as I look at the territory of my people
around the foot of Errigal

where they've settled
for more than three hundred years
on the grassy mountain pastures
from Mín 'a Leá to Mín na Craoibhe.
Here before me, open
like a book,
is this countryside now
from Doire Chonaire to Prochlais.
Above and below, I see the holdings
farmed from the mouth of wilderness.
This is the poem-book of my people,
the manuscript they toiled at
with the ink of their sweat.
Here every enclosed field is like a verse
in the great poem of land reclamation.
I now read this epic of diligence
in the green dialect of the holdings,
understand that I'm only fulfilling my duty
when I challenge the void
exactly as my people challenged the wilderness
with diligence and devotion
till they earned their prize.
Here I feel the worth of poetry
I feel my *raison d'être* and importance as a person
as I become the pulse of my people's heart
and from this certainty comes peace of mind.
My desires are tamed, my thoughts mellow,
contradictions are cancelled on the spot.

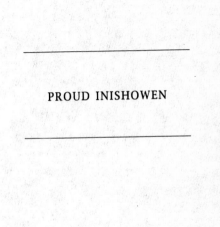

PROUD INISHOWEN

The Girl from Glenagivney

Anonymous

Glenagivney is a long and beautiful glen that leads to Kinnagoe Bay on the north coast. Greencstle and Magilligan are at opposite ends of the mouth of Lough Foyle.

'Twas on a Monday morning, in weather calm and clear,
I crossed Greencastle ferry, in springtime of the year;
I crossed Greencastle ferry free from all care and toil,
To view the hills and valleys across the river Foyle.

Magilligan's a neat wee place and that full well is known,
But I intend to leave it and live in Inishowen.
Where pretty girls are found galore, as everyone can see
Above all parts of Ireland sweet Inishowen for me.

The road to Glenagivney is above Greencastle town;
There lives a handsome colleen of honour and renown;
The smiles of her bright countenance have so enchanted me,
By Cupid's dart I've found the smart, I'm wounded quite by she.

'I'm sorry, miss, you slight me, and I your wounded slave;
I'll never cease to worship you until I reach my grave;
Perhaps you'll rue't when I'm far off; when Cupid sets me free;
So take kind Fortune as your guide and come and marry me.'

'The character I got of you, it pleases me right well;
I care not what my friends may think, I'm out to please
    mysel'.
And if the Fates are kind at all, we'll lead a happy life;
So I have no objection, John, I'll be your loving wife.'

The Blazing Star of Drung

Anonymous

Drung is a tiny loughside village about fifteen miles from Derry on the Moville
road.

The first time that I saw my love, the stormy winds did blow;
The hills and dales and valleys were covered o'er with snow;
I being too late a friend to treat which caused me to stray,
Where I beheld that bonny wee lass that stole my heart away.

The next time that I saw my love, she smiled and passed me by
Says I to her, 'My bonny wee lass, where does your dwelling
    lie?'
She answered me right modestly with kind and mild a tongue,
Kind sir, my habitation and my dwelling lie in Drung.

I courted her the lee long night and part of the next day;
I could wish wi' all my heart I had her on the say;
I asked her off her brother John; he said she was too young;
Till the day I die I'll ne'er deny that I loved the maid of Drung.

Oh, Nancy, you're my fancy; you're my only joy and care;
Your parents they were angry and would not let me near;
It's not your gold or silver that I would value a pin;
I'd maintain you like a lady if you were far from Drung.

My love she's like the morning star; she dresses all by day;
Her lovely neck and shoulders they excel the lilies gay;
Her charming voice made me rejoice, she sung her notes so
    clear;
I would count it next to paradise to be with you, my dear.

It's farewell Londonderry, it was there I learned my trade;
And likewise to Dungiven where I was born and bred;
Here's a health to my wee darling, our ship is going on,
And twice farewell to that bonny wee lass – she's the blazing
    star of Drung.

The Wreck of the *Saldhana*

Thomas Sheridan

Thomas Sheridan was the son of Richard Brinsley Sheridan, the great
dramatist, and father of Helen, Lady Dufferin, the poet. The *Saldhana* sank
in Lough Swilly on 4 December 1811 with the loss of all hands.

'Rule Britannia' sang the crew
When the stout *Saldhana* sailed,
And her colours as they flew
Flung the warrior cross to view

Which in battle to subdue
   Ne'er had failed.

From the lonely beacon's height
As the watchman gazed around,
They saw that flashing light
Drive swift athwart the night,
Yet the wind was fair and right
   For the sound.

But no mortal power shall now
That crew and vessel save –
They are shrouded as they go
In a hurricane of snow
And the track beneath the prow
   Is their grave.

Oe'r Swilly rocks they soar,
Commissioned watch to keep;
Down, down with thundering roar,
The exulting Demons pour –
The *Saldhana* floats no more
   On the deep.

'Britannia rules the wave!'
Ah! vain and impious boast!
Go mark, presumptuous slaves,
Where He, who sinks or saves,
Scars the sands with countless graves
   Round your coast.

Inis-Eoghain

Charles Gavan Duffy

Charles Gavan Duffy, born in Monaghan in 1816, was the first editor of the *Nation*. in which this poem appeared. He emigrated to Australia, became prime minister of Victoria in 1871 and was knighted in 1873. He died in France in 1903.

God bless the grey mountains of dark Dún na nGall,
God bless royal Aileach, the pride of them all;
For she sits evermore like a queen on her throne,
And smiles on the valleys of green Inis-Eoghain,
    And fair are the valleys of green Inis-Eoghain,
    And hardy the fishers, that can call them their own.
    A race that nor traitor nor coward have known
    Enjoy the valleys of green Inis-Eoghain.

Oh! simple and bold are the bosoms they bear,
Like the hills that with silence and nature they share,
For our God, who hath planted our home near his own,
Breathed His spirit abroad upon fair Inis-Eoghain,
    Then praise to our Father for wild Inis-Eoghain,
    Where fiercely forever the surges are thrown –
    Nor weather nor fortune a tempest hath blown
    Could shake the strong bosoms of brave Inis-Eoghain.

See the beautiful Couldah careering along –
A type of their manhood so stately and strong –
On the weary forever its tide is bestown,

So they share with the stranger in fair Inis-Eoghain.
    God guard the kind homesteads of fair Inis-Eoghain
    Which manhood and virtue have chosen for their own;
    Not long shall the nation in slavery groan,
    That rears the tall peasants of fair Inis-Eoghain.

Like the oak of St Bride which nor Devil nor Dane,
Nor Saxon nor Dutchman could rend from her fane,
They have clung by the creed and the cause of their own
Through the midnight of danger in true Inis-Eoghain.
    Then shout for the glories of old Inis-Eoghain,
    The stronghold that foemen have never o'erthrown –
    The soul and the spirit, the blood and the bone,
    That guard the green valleys of true Inis-Eoghain.

Nor purer of old was the tongue of the Gael,
When the charging *aboo* made the foreigner quail,
Than it gladdens the stranger in welcome's soft tone
In the home-loving cabins of kind Inis-Eoghain.
    Oh! flourish ye homesteads of kind Inis-Eoghain
    Where seeds of a people's redemption are sown;
    Right soon shall the fruit of that sowing have grown,
    To bless the kind homesteads of green Inis-Eoghain.

When they tell us a tale of a spell-stricken band,
All entranced, with their bridles and broad swords in hand,
Who await but the word to give Erin her own,
They can read you that riddle in proud Inis-Eoghain.
    Hurra for the spaemen of proud Inis-Eoghain!
    Long live the wild Seers of stout Inis-Eoghain,
    May Mary, our mother, be deaf to our moan
    Who love not the promise of proud Inis-Eoghain!

The Lake of Shadows

Cecil Frances Alexander

Cecil Frances Alexander was born in Dublin in 1818 but moved to Strabane at the age of fifteen. It was here that she wrote the hymns for which she is still famous. After her marriage to Rev William Alexander she lived in Castlederg and Fahan, and Derry when her husband became bishop. This poem about Lough Swilly was the first to comment upon its magical light.

I stood beside the shadowy lake.
　　I watch'd the glorious brimful tide
In lines of foamy music break
　　Against her shingly side.

The wild hills, by her waters kissed,
　　Hung round her soft as soft might be;
They glimmered through a silver mist
　　Down on a silver sea.

And, where their darkest ridge upheaves,
　　A rich red light was streaming o'er -
Like a great heap of crimson leaves
　　Piled on a purple floor.

Red in the western heaven on high,
　　Red in the burning lake below,
And deep-red in the eastern sky,
　　That kindled with the glow.

The Hurricane

John Keys O'Doherty DD

JK O'Doherty was born in Derry in 1833 and was made bishop in 1889. He
wrote the catechism that was used for many years in the diocese. An
antiquarian, he wrote much occasional verse. He died in 1907.

The summer's sun was sinking down 'neath Binion's waveless
   bay,
And burnishing its rippling tide with many a golden ray;
The zephyrs stayed their wanton steps, and hushed their
   every breath –
The scene was still, the bay was bright and undisturbed as
   death.
Tall Raghlin looked with queenly pride far out into the main,
And Binion threw its giant shade across the watery plain;
And fair Donaff in distance blue raised up its head on high,
And caught the sun's expiring beams, and kissed the
   cloudless sky –
No dark spot dimm'd the broad expanse that spann'd the
   silent sea;
That sky was fair as eastern bride, and brighter far than she!

A tiny boat, like speck of snow, on ocean's bosom hoar,
Had spread its sails at early morn, and left that lonely shore;
The noontide sun had seen it far out on the watery track,
And vesper lit her dazzling lamp to guide the wanderer back.
The idle sails now flap the mast, no breeze disturbs the sea,

And through Lagg Bar the angry tide for once steals silently;
The boatmen press the pliant oars, and raise the jocund song –
They pass the tower of Malin Head girt round by barriers
    strong;
And Tullagh's strand is full in view, and seen is rough
    Maymore –
Full well these boatmen know each spot from Doagh to
    Leenan Shore!

But just athwart the day-god's track a sudden gloom has
    passed,
As if the night her sombre veil across the day had cast;
A vivid flash lights up that gloom, the sudden thunder rolls –
It peals along the startled heavens, and roars around the
    poles.
The gushing rain comes dancing forth in drenching torrents
    wild,
And leaps the whirlwind from its throne of storms on storm-
    clouds piled,
It sweeps the main with tyrant might – upheaves the tranquil
    bay –
And dashes o'er the troubled sea like dolphin at its play;
It crests the wave with snowy foam, throws billows mountain
    high,
And rears up watery spires that pierce the bosom of the sky!

The storm has ceased, the night is on, and sighs the dying gale,
And quick the swollen streamlets run in murmurs down the
    vale;
And where's the boat – poor tiny thing – that rode the waves at
    morn,
And spread in pride its snowy sail like butterfly just born?

And where's the crew that mann'd that boat – Clonmany's
seamen bold –
Who feared no tide, disdained all storms, felt not the
winter's cold?
They've sunk beneath the billow's breast, down in the salt-
sea wave –
No humble cross in hallowed spot shall mark their lonely
grave.
Their shroud shall be the sea-weed green, their tomb the
ocean sand,
Their epitaph – the tale which tells their fate upon the land.

The summer's sun again looks down on Binion's waveless
bay,
And sees no trace which marks the storm that swept it
yesterday;
But there are hearts beneath that tide cold, cold as winter's
snow,
Which never more shall feel life's joys, nor taste its cup of
woe.
On yester-morn those hearts were glad – their life blood
bounded free –
The tempest swept across the deep, and sunk them in the
sea!
There shall they sleep regarding not the storms that o'er
them rave;
No sound of busy life shall break the stillness of their grave;
Eternal hurricanes may roll unheeded o'er their head –
No voice they'll hear but that which cries:– 'Arise, arise ye
dead!'

The Horsemen of Aileach

Alice Milligan

Alice Milligan was born near Omagh in 1865 and after a spell of teaching in Derry edited with Ethna Carbery the *Northern Patriot* and the *Shan Van Vocht*. She died in 1953. The poem, an obvious tribute to Pearse, refers to the legend that the warriors of Hugh O'Neill lie asleep near Grianan of Aileach waiting for the summons to set Ireland free.

'Tis told in tales of wonder how Aileach's palace under
Kings in countless number lie still as carven stone;
And steeds with them in hiding are reined for warriors'
   riding
To the last of Erin's battles from that cave of Inish Owen.

And once in summer's shining, on Fahan's shore reclining,
The hissing of the heather and the droning of the sea,
And the lisp of wavelets creeping, they lulled my brain to
   sleeping,
And the glory of that story in a vision burst on me.

In the moments of my slumber, years I seemed to number,
Centuries flew by like the down of thistle light;
And through gloom of Slavery's sadness, my heart still leapt
   for gladness
Or throbbed in wild impatience for the ages' swifter flight.

I knew (God's angel told it) mine eyes should yet behold it,
Though patriots' blood in torrents poured and martyrs' like a
    shower,
Our Erin's resurrection from the tomb of long subjection,
And the dawn from gulfs of darkness of her freedom's
    shining hour.

I knew through years of weeping how the caverned hill was
    keeping
The most valiant of our chieftains in a trance-sleep still and
    dumb,
'Neath the ferns and grasses waving, for the hour Erin's
    saving,
And but waiting for the summons of one nobler yet to come.

Then when stars wheeled down and whitened, as the rose of
    sunrise brightened,
A wind along the ocean came rushing to my ear;
And through roar of billows drumming, softly whispered, '*He
is coming,*'
Then a call along the mountain rang, announcing, '*He is
here!*'

Oh, in that hour of wonder the air was thrilled by thunder
And like a sword unsheathing the cloud flung up the flame,
And with crash of hillside rending, through shattered rocks
    descending
To the last of Erin's battles the host of Aileach came.

One led in royal splendour, his face in grace most tender,
His voice like battle's trumpet-blast, his hand unmatched in
    might;

His deeds shed fame victorious on a name by far more glorious
Then the name of all the noblest that e'er strove for Erin's
    right.

They passed – and all my dreaming was then of falchions
    gleaming,
Of valleys loud with shouting, and of rivers flowing red,
Of the Saxon sea-ward flying, amidst heaps of vanquished
    dying,
And the sunburst banner floating o'er a youthful conqueror's
    head.

Then at hush of battle thunder, a cry of joy and wonder
Went up from warriors thronging round a leader no man
    knew:
'Who are thou,' the chieftains shouted, 'who the Saxon host
    hast routed?
'Who art thou who waked and led us?' and the hillsides
    echoed 'Who?'

The Buncrana Train

Anon

This song first published in the Derry Journal in 1898 was still being sung in 1949 when the L&LSR finally closed.

Some people like to have a drive
Whilst others like a row,
Young people getting up in life
A-courting they will go.
But if the evening does keep fine
And does not threaten rain,
Sure I'd prefer a trip to Fahan
On the Buncrana train
Chorus

For Crockett he's the driver,
And Bonner is the guard,
And if you have a ticket
All care you can discard.
Let you be fop or summer swell
To them it's all the same,
For every man must pay it's fare
On the Buncrana train

For localists, provocalists,
And those that like to sing,
I'm sure McGarvey he'll be there
To play the Highland Fling.
As for singing or for dancing

To them it's all the same,
For he's the sole 'musicianer'
On the Buncrana train.
Chorus

We pass Bridgend, reach Burnfoot,
And there we give a call
To view that ancient city
And its Corporation Hall.
The King of Tory Island
Is a man of widespread fame,
His Royal Carriage is attached
To the Buncrana train.
Chorus

We go to Fahan to have a dip
And stroll along the strand,
The up the road to have a cup
Of coffee at the Stand.
The barmaid she is charming,
With her you can remain
Until it's time for to go back
On the Buncrana train.
Chorus

HIGHLANDS AND ISLANDS

The Rose of Aranmore

Anonymous

A tribute in waltz time to Donegal's largest island.

My thoughts today, though I'm far away,
Dwell on Tyrconnell's shore,
The salt sea air and the colleens fair
Of lovely green Gweedore.
There's a flower there, beyond compare,
That I'll treasure ever more,
That grand colleen, in her gown of green,
She's the Rose of Aranmore.

I've travelled far 'neath the Northern star,
Since the day I said goodbye;
And seen many maids in the golden glades
Beneath a tropic sky.
There's a vision in my reverie,
I always will adore,
That grand colleen, in her gown of green,
She's the Rose of Aranmore.

But soon I will return again
To the scenes I loved so well,
Where many an Irish lad and lass
Their tales of love do tell;
The silvery dunes and blue lagoons,
Along the Rosses shore

And that grand colleen, in her gown of green,
She's the Rose of Aranmore.

Wild Donegal
from *Ireland, its Scenery, Characters, etc*
A. M. and S. C. Hall

Anna Maria Fielding, born in Dublin in 1800, was the author of many novels and plays. She married Samuel Carter Hall in 1824 and together they wrote the best account of pre-famine Ireland. She died in 1881 in East Mousley.

Along this coast too is Torry Island, which is inhabited by about five hundred persons, the greater number of whom have never visited the mainland. Some few years ago a few of its fishermen were driven on shore, and when they returned to their island homes they took with them leaves of trees as the greatest curiosity they could show to their people. Here also is a town buried beneath the sand; here, until of late years, the illicit distiller carried on his trade without the remotest dread of interruption, and the whiskey of Inishowen became proverbial for its excellence. Indeed, the coast from Moville round to Killybegs was famous for all that was rude, uncultivated and lawless.

The northern and western districts of Donegal afford rich materials for a volume. Our own journey however lies southward to Donegal Bay through a remarkably wild country, which is magnificent in the extreme, although it is infinitely less so than the rude coasts which keep out the Atlantic.

From Londonderry we verged westward to the ancient city

of Raphoe, returning by the direct route to Donegal and so visiting the town of Stranorlar and the border town of Strabane. On our way through St Johnstown we visited a singular lake, Fort Lough, where there has always been a tradition that this lake (in common with many other lakes in Ireland) had a castle erected in the centre of the water beneath the waves. This tradition was long considered fanciful; however, as twenty years ago an attempt was made to reclaim the morass, and as the waters of the lake subsided, marks of an island became visible in the centre. By degrees regular masonry was observed ascending above the surface, and there can now be seen, even from the road, the remains of a building at the bottom of the lake, proving that the subaquatic castle was no visionary fiction, but a real existence.

————

The maritime county of Donegal in the province of Ulster is bounded on the east and south-east by the counties of Londonderry, Tyrone and Fermanagh. (It is separated from Londonderry by Lough Foyle.) It is bounded on the south by Donegal Bay, the northern extremity of the county of Leitrim, and on the north and west by the Atlantic Ocean.

It is divided into the baronies of Raphoe, Kilmacrenan, Inishowen, Tyrhugh, Bannagh and Boylagh. Its principal towns are Donegal, Ballyshannon, Killybegs, Lifford, Letterkenny, St Johnstown and Stranorlar.

On the Road to Glen-Columcille
From *Mearing Stones*
Joseph Campbell

Campbell's book is subtitled 'Leaves from my Note-Book on Tramp in Donegal (1911)'.

We reach the high-road in about half-an-hour, near a school-house, shining white in the sun, and busy with the hum of children singing over their lessons. Things look more familiar now. We pass many houses, with fleeces of dyed wool – green and blue and madder – drying on bushes outside the doors, and men busy stacking turf and thatching. Here and there on the road flocks of geese lie sunning themselves, head-under-wing. As we draw near they get up and face us with protruding necks, hissing viciously. Dogs bark at us occasionally, but not often. (I had heard ill accounts of the Donegal dogs from travellers, but on the whole, my experience of them had not been quite so bad as I had been led to expect.) Slieve League rises on our left, a dark, shadowy bulk of mountain, shutting off the view to the south. All around is moorland, with a stream in spate foaming through a depression in it, and little patches of tilled land here and there, and the inevitable brown-thatched cabin and the peat-reek over it. After some miles' travelling we come on a little folk-shop by the road – a shop where one might buy anything from a clay-pipe or a lemon to Napoleon's Book of Fate. The window looks tempting, so we go in. The shopkeeper is a quiet-mannered little man, not very old, I would think, but with greyish hair, and eyes that looked as if they were bound round with red tape – burnt out of his head with snuff and peat-smoke. We ask him has he any buttermilk to sell. He hasn't any, unfortunately – he is just run out of it – so we content ourselves with Derry biscuits, made up in penny cartons, and half-a-dozen hen-eggs to suck on the way. Some people may shiver at the idea of it, but raw eggs are as sustaining a thing as one could take on a journey! We pay our score, and get under way again. At a bridge where the road forks we sit down and eat our simple repast. A bridge has always a peculiar fascination for me – especially in an open country like this where one's horizon is not limited by trees and hedges – and I could spend hours dawdling over it, watching the play of sun and shadow on the water as it foams away under the arches. Here there is a delightful sense of space and quietness. The heather-ale is in our hearts, the water sings and the wind blows, and one ceases to trouble about time and the multitude of petty vexations that worry the townsman out of happiness. Did I say one ceases to trouble about time? Even here it comes, starting one like a guilty thing. We reach Meenacross Post-office at four-thirty, and an hour later see the Atlantic tumbling through rain on the age-worn strand of Glen-Columcille.

I met an old man on the road, and his face as yellow as dyer's rocket. 'Walk easy past that little house beyond,' says he in a whisper, turning round and pointing with his staff into the valley. 'There's a young girl in it, and she celebrating the festival of death.'

The Price of Flour
From *Islanders*
Peadar O'Donnell

Peadar O'Donnell was born near Dungloe in 1893 and taught in several of
the islands of the Rosses before becoming a trade union organiser especially
among the migrant workers in Scotland. An active socialist, he wrote in all
seven novels and much journalism, and was the founder of the famous mid-
century journal *The Bell*. He died in 1986.

When the mother got to her feet she gathered the skins and
broken potatoes into the dish and bruised them for the hens.
Then having cleared the table she stood for a moment with her
hands resting on her hips, her eyes fixed again on the fire. She
sighed a deep sigh and turned to the dresser. Pushing the plates
aside she took a small paper packet from the back of the shelf
and, opening it, counted the coppers it held. Her eyes went to
the eleven eggs on the dresser. She tapped her unbroken front
teeth with her thumb. She put the coppers back. She took up
the dish of hens' meat: she threw it out in handfuls, calling the
hens softly the while.

A light patter of bare feet sounded behind her. Without
turning she said: 'Come here, Hughie.'

The lad who had run over to Mary Manus came to her side.
That he was her son was evident at the first gaze. There was
the same open countenance, the same large grey eyes, strangely
filled with understanding for a boy so young. There was
eagerness now and joy in his face.

'Neddy's dog got the duck egg last night again,' she said.

'It was my fault,' he said, the joy ebbing.

The mother turned towards him, the trace of a passing smile lighting her face for a moment. Without speaking she went into the house. Hughie followed her in.

'There's ninepence in coppers there,' she said, 'an' there's eleven eggs. Ye could get the loan of an egg from Peggy to make the dozen. They're tenpence the day. That'ud be nineteen pence. Flour's elevenpence a half stone, an' a quarter of tay id be sixpence. But tay without sugar id be little use.'

'I got a lobster,' Hughie said, the glow that had been crushed out returning to his face.

'A lobster,' the mother said, almost as excited as himself. 'Aye,' he said nodding eagerly. 'I caught him in the hole behind the black rock. I gave him to Neil Jack. He gave me sevenpence.' He opened his fist and exposed a sixpence and a penny.

'Well, glory be to God,' the mother exclaimed, 'if that doesn't beat the wee wheel. Away with ye and get the egg from Peggy. Ye'll have threepence halfpenny left after the sugar.'

Hughie went out and over to Peggy's, his married sister's. Peggy was out, but the eggs were in a row on the dresser. He took one and hurried back home.

'Ye'll catch the boat yet over at the West Bay,' the mother said. 'Get a stone of flour, a quarter of tay, and a pound of sugar. That leaves threepence halfpenny. We'll get Charlie an ounce of tobacco. He hadn't a good smoke this week. That leaves a halfpenny.'

'That'll get snuff for yerself,' Hughie said.

'Bad cess to it for snuff,' she said. 'Sheila spilled half of the last on me. I'm run out. Maybe we'd as well get another halfpenny worth. Steal away without them seeing ye. We'll give them all a surprise at tea-time. A mhic, an' mind ye don't fall with the eggs.'

She handed him the eggs in a handkerchief. A blush suffused the boy's features. The mother noticed it.

'Well, I'll tell ye what,' she said. 'I'll put the eggs into a can, an' nobody'll know what ye have. Them that'd make fun of ye for takin' eggs to the shop id have little to do. But anyway, this is the best way, an' ye can take the tay and sugar back in the can.'

She watched him as he tripped across the green. Then she took out her snuff-box and emptied it recklessly on the back of her hand and sniffed eagerly.

Tory
From *The Islands of Ireland*
Thomas H. Mason

Like most of the western islands Tory is treeless, and the side facing the Atlantic is bounded by high cliffs. These cliffs are worn into fantastic pillars of rock or tors, from which the island takes its name. I need hardly say the name has no connection with a modern political party.

———

The inhabitants of Tory frequently live to a great age. At the time of my visit one man was a hundred years old and was looking for another wife. In former years they elected a 'king'. The last king was a very small man, as his tiny chair indicates, and he must have possessed a powerful personality to compensate for his diminutive stature.

It is easy to understand persistence of tradition and the spoken word in a long-living, primitive and isolated community, and nowhere have I observed this emphasised so strongly as on Tory Island. Prehistoric myths and legends are mixed up with events of medieval history and recent happenings, and the whole jumble is narrated as if were a single tale of the occurrences of a few years ago. The predominating figure of the mythology of the island is Balor, the God Chief of the Fomorians, a race of legendary pirates who inhabited the island in early times and from their stronghold scourged the rest of Ireland with their depredations. Balor was a most unpleasant gentleman; he had an eye, like Cyclops, in the front of his head, and so wicked was he that an angry glance from his single eye was sufficient to slay the beholder. When his eye became tired in battle the eyelid was held up by means of ropes and pulleys so that his followers would not lose the advantage of his deadly glance.

———

The present head of the Dugan family is a dignified old man named Anthony. Only the head of the family has 'the power' and I know of cases where people travelled sixty miles to obtain 'Tory clay' from him. I first heard of this clay from a postmaster in County Donegal who emphasised the fact that he was not superstitious. He had tried traps and poison to get rid of the pests, but without result, so, in desperation, he made the journey to Tory, obtained the clay, and a week after he had sprinkled it around their holes not a rat was to be seen or heard. They had vanished.

———

I was troubled with rats in my works and had made inquiries how I could obtain the clay, as I was anxious to test its power on the Dublin rats. At the door of his house I knocked and asked for Anthony. I was brought into the living-room where, seated near the fire, was an old man who told me he was Anthony Dugan. I made my request as previously instructed: 'In the name of God give me some Tory clay.'

He regarded me keenly for a few moments and then bade me be seated. Rising, he took a small paper bag from his bedroom and went out, proceeding to the ruins of a small church about fifty yards away. When he arrived at the interior of the church he knelt down and said a prayer. Then he took a couple of handfuls of clay and put them in the paper bag which he handed to me in the house. I was much impressed by the whole proceeding, which was reverent and dignified.

Unfortunately when I came home from my holidays the rats had disappeared, and when they returned after a couple of years I could not find the paper bag in which the clay was contained.

Dawn in Inishtrahull

D. J. O'S

Daniel James O'Sullivan was born in Cork in 1906 and worked with Irish Lights. He was stationed for many years in Inishtrahull, north of Malin Head, and became a distinguished field naturalist. He died in Dublin in 1994.

The moon shines on the Isle of Inishtrahull,
Bejewelling nuptial tinted herring-gull,
May-fly dancing in the balmy air,
And moth returning to its daylight lair.

A shoal of herring breaking out at sea
Sparkle like hoar-frost on an aspen tree,

Spindrift in the shaded rocky cleft,
And raised-beach quartz that the ice-ages left.

The droning beetles seek the crevassed walls
To dive into when hungry lapwing calls;
Earwigs, likewise, into earthed homes,
And red-ants under scarred lichened stones.

An otter seeking rest on rock remote
Glistens with phosphorescence on his coat,
The snail *Arborum*, with his watery glue,
And bunch of pearlwort in a crystal dew.

The flaming sun ascends o'er Cantyre's Mull,
Flings out his arms, day breaks on Inishtrahull!

An Leacht Mór
From *The Secret Places of Donegal*
John M. Feehan

John Feehan was born in Cashel in 1916 and, after a military career in which he attained to the rank of captain, founded the Mercier Press, for which he wrote many books. He died in 1991.

I went north from Burtonport and made a little diversion to the left out to Cruit island. It is not really an island since it is connected to the mainland by a bridge. Cruit island is another of the secret places of Donegal. Here you have magnificent peaceful beaches, unusually uncrowded. It is also a great place for holy wells, which a local cynic told me are being added to every year! So if you had a shovel handy you could dig one for yourself. Scatter a few ribbons and medals around and no doubt some archaeologist will find a connection between it and Balor of the Evil Eye.

There is also a large slab on Cruit island called An *Leacht Mór* which is said to cure illness if you sleep on it. I would imagine, however, if you could possibly sleep on it you couldn't be very sick. A thirsty talkative tourist, whom I once met in a pub, explained to me that the slab was really a fertility rock. For childless couples, he said, to exercise their conjugal rights here worked miracles. Indeed he was certain that scores of Donegal people owed their existence to a summer frolic on An *Leacht Mór*. So if you have a little problem it might be worth a try. It couldn't do much harm anyway.

East of Cruit island is the little village of Annagry where the people have a reputation for being tightlipped and uncommunicative. There is a story told of an Annagry man who, while on pilgrimage to Rome, attended a sermon preached by the Pope.

'What did he preach about?' he was asked when he came home.

'Sin.'

'What did he have to say about it?'

'I'd say he was against it,' was the laconic answer.

I did not find the people of Annagry particularly uncommunicative. Indeed they were most helpful to me when I enquired the way to the remote townsland of Kerrytown. I was given precise and exact directions which enabled me to find the place without trouble.

Kerrytown became famous during the Second World War, because the Blessed Virgin was supposed to have appeared many times there. According to local testimony she was a very beautiful lady in her early twenties. She wore a magnificent blue robe and a wreath of flowers on her head. She carried a curly-haired baby in her arms. She appeared several times to many people, including a very sceptical priest. Because of newspaper reports Kerrytown became a place of pilgrimage and thousands flocked there to pray especially on feastdays of the Blessed Virgin.

In later years the fervour seems to have eased off and the day I went to visit it it was deserted. An unusual framed picture of the Blessed Virgin was resting on a rock in the cliff and scattered around were some small statues, medals, money and ribbons. Yet as I sat alone in the heather, I felt a strange prayerful atmosphere all around the place – much more prayerful than I ever felt at Lourdes or Knock. A kind of an untroubled calm descended on my soul. It was as if there were no evil in the world – only immense goodness, like Eden before the fall.

SONGS AND STORIES

The Star of Donegal

Anonymous

One evening fair to take the air, alone I chanced to stray
Down by a limpid silv'ry stream that flows beside the way.
I heard two lovers talking by an ancient ruined hall
And the fair one's name was Mary Jane, the Star of Donegal.

'My lovely maid,' the youth he said, 'I'm going across the foam
Unto the land of stars and stripes where peace and plenty flows
I want your faithful promise that you'll wed with none at all
Until I do return to you and the lands of Donegal.'

She blushed and sighed and then replied: 'It grieves my heart
    full sore,
To think you are compelled to go and leave the Shamrock
    shore.
Here is my faithful promise that I'll wed with none at all
But stay at home and do not roam from the lands of
    Donegal.'

'My sweet fair maid,' the youth then said, 'at home I cannot
    stay;
To California's gold-fields I'm bound to cross the sea
To accumulate a fortune great and build a splendid hall,
To decorate and cultivate the lands of Donegal.'

She raised her lily-white hands and said: 'Yon castle in its
   day,
With all its plains and large demesnes from Lifford to the sea
Belonged to our ancestors with many a splendid hall,
And if my father had his rights, I'd be heir of Donegal.'

'My darling maid,' the youth then said, 'the day is drawing
   near,
When Irishmen will return again from all their long career,
Our holy land by God's command the fairest land of all,
And Heaven will see old Ireland free, Bright Star of Donegal.'

She blushed and sighed and then replied: 'Heaven grant that
   we may see
Saint Patrick's isle of Saints to shine great, glorious and free.
If that be so there's none will go to New York or Montreal,
But stay at home and will not roam from the lands of
   Donegal.

He clasped her in his arms and said, 'My darling, well you
   know
I love you very dearly and loth I am to go.
Let us get wed without fear or dread, that puts an end to all
And then I will have my darling girl the Star of Donegal.'

She gave consent and off they went to meet with Father
   Hugh,
Who joined their hands in wedlock bands without any more
   ado.
From Derry quay they sailed away and bade farewell to all,
And now they're in America, far away from Donegal.

Oh! The Praties They Are Small Over Here

Anonymous

This poem appeared in the *Midland Tribune* more than a hundred years ago but it seems to me to belong to Donegal.

Oh! the Praties they are small over here - over here,
Oh! the Praties they are small over here,
Oh! the Praties they are small and we dug them in the fall,
And we ate them skins and all, full of fear - full of fear.

Oh! I wish that we were geese in the morn - in the morn,
Oh! I wish that we were geese in the morn,
Oh! I wish that we were geese, for they live and die in peace,
Till the hour of their decease, eatin' corn - eatin' corn.

Oh! we're down into the dust, over here - over here
Oh! we're down into the dust over here,
Oh! we're down into the dust, but the Lord in whom we trust,
Will soon give us crumb or crust over here - over here.

The Girl from Donegal

Anon

Song made popular (like many others) by Delia Murphy (1902–71)

Young girls draw near and I'll tell you here
The news that makes me sad,
He sailed away the other day,
My own dear Irish lad,
My heart did break all for his sake
And tears like rain did fall,
Ah, why did he part and break the heart
Of his girl from Donegal.

He was big and strong; when he'd sing a song
He'd delight your heart to hear,
With the step so light and his eyes so bright
And his voice so sweet and clear,
He could handle a spade or court a maid,
The fairest of them all,
But he was inclined to leave behind
His girl from Donegal.

The weather was bad and my love was sad
The day that he sailed away,
To a distant land across the foam
In a foreign land to slave.
He would rather have toiled on his native soil,

But his wages were too small,
That's why he did part and break the heart
Of his girl from Donegal.

I wished in vain he would remain,
But he had to sail away,
And he left me here to pine and fear
Till he'd return some day,
But if this time he doesn't want to,
He needn't return at all,
For why did he part and break the heart
Of his girl from Donegal.

I'm Going to Buncrana
'T. B.'

Apart from the fact than he/she was from Derry nothing else is known about 'T. B.'.

Without you I feel weary,
The day seems long and dreary,
I miss your voice so cheery,
          My little Swilly Rose;
Then, farewell care and sorrow,
A day from toil I'll borrow
And meet you, dear, tomorrow
          Where old Mill River flows.

Chorus

I'm going to Buncrana,
To see my fair Roseanna,
She's brighter than Diana,
    She's all the world to me.
Her graceful form so slender,
Her voice so sweet and tender,
Her smiling eyes in splendour
    Have charms divine to see.

She sings till 'Encore' after,
Brings loud applause and laughter,
Admirers seek her, dafter,
    Their compliments to pay:
They're all so fond of Rosie,
She looks so neat and cosy;
My darlin' she's a 'posie',
    And I know she's OK.

The Last Friends

Frances Browne

Frances Browne was born in Stranorlar in 1816. Blind from infancy because of smallpox, she still managed to attend school and became a well-known writer. Her collection of fairy stories, *Granny's Wonderful Chair* is still a children's classic. She died in 1879. This poem is put in the mouth of a returned political exile.

I came to my country, but not with the hope
    That brightened my youth like the cloud-lighting bow
For the region of soul that seemed mighty to cope
    With time and with fortune, hath fled from me now;
And love, that illumined my wanderings of yore,
    Hath perished, and left but a weary regret
For the star that can rise on my midnight no more –
    But the hills of my county they welcome me yet!

The hue of their verdure was fresh with me still,
    When my path was afar by the Tanais' lone track;
From the wide-spreading deserts and ruins that fill
    The land of old story, they summoned me back;
They rose on my dreams through the shades of the west,
    They breathed upon sands which the dew never wet,
For the echoes were hushed in the home I loved best –
    But I knew that the mountains would welcome me yet!

The dust of my kindred is scattered afar,
     They lie in the desert, the wild, and the wave;
For serving the strangers through wandering and war,
     The isle of their memory could grant them no grave,
And I, I return with the memory of years,
     Whose hope rose so high though its sorrow is set;
They have left on my soul but the trace of their tears –
     But our mountains remember their promises yet!

Oh! where are the brave hearts that bounded of old,
     And where are the faces my childhood hath seen?
For fair brows are furrowed, and hearts have grown cold,
     But our streams are still bright, and our hills are still
     green;
Ay, green as they rose to the eyes of my youth,
     When brothers in heart in their shadows we met;
And the hills have no memory of sorrow or death,
     For their summits are sacred to liberty yet!

Like ocean retiring, the morning mists now
     Roll back from the mountains that girdle our land;
And sunlight encircles each heath-covered brow
     For which time had no furrow and tyrants no brand!
Oh, thus let it be with the hearts of the isle,
     Efface the dark seal that oppression hath set;
Give back the lost glory again to the soil,
     For the hills of my country remember it yet!

The Memory of the Dead

John Kells Ingram

John Kells Ingram was born near Pettigo in 1823 and educated at Trinty where he later held the chair of Greek. He died in 1907.

Who fears to speak of Ninety-eight?
Who blushes at the name?
When cowards mock the patriot's fate,
Who hangs his head for shame?
He's all a knave, or half a slave,
Who slights his country thus;
But a true man, like you, man,
Will fill your glass with us.

We drink the memory of the brave,
The faithful and the few;
Some lie far off beyond the wave,
Some sleep in Ireland, too;
All, all are gone; but still lives on
The fame of those who died;
All true men, like you, men,
Remember them with pride.

Some on the shores of distant lands
Their weary hearts have laid,
And by the stranger's heedless hands
Their lonely graves were made;
But though their clay be far away

Beyond the Atlantic foam,
In true men, like you, men,
Their spirit's still at home.

The dust of some is Irish earth,
Among their own they rest,
And the same land that gave them birth
Has caught them to her breast;
And we will pray that from their clay
Full many a race may start
Of true men, like you, men
To act as brave a part.

They rose in dark and evil days
To right their native land;
They kindled here a living blaze
That nothing shall withstand.
Alas! that might can vanquish right –
They fell and passed away;
But true men, like you, men
Are plenty here to-day.

Then here's their memory – may it be
For us a guiding light,
To cheer our strife for liberty,
And teach us to unite –
Through good and ill, be Ireland's still,
Though sad as theirs your fate,
And true men be you, men,
Like those of Ninety-eight.

O'Donnell Aboo

M. J. McCann

Michael Joseph McCann was born in Galway in 1824 and after teaching in Tuam took up journalism in London where he died in 1883. This famous poem was written for the *Nation* and celebrates the O'Donnell victory at Ballyshannon in 1597.

Proudly the note of the trumpet is sounding,
Loudly the war-cries arise on the gale;
Fleetly the steed by Lough Swilly is bounding,
To join the thick squadrons in Saimear's green vale.
    On ev'ry mountaineer
    Strangers to flight and fear!
Rush to the standard of dauntless Red Hugh!
    Bonnaught and gallowglass,
    Throng from each mountain pass
On for old Erin, 'O'Donnell Aboo!'

Princely O'Neill to our aid is advancing
With many a chieftain and warrior clan,
A thousand steeds in his vanguard are prancing
'Neath the borderers brave from the banks of the Bann;
    Many a heart shall quail
    Under his coat of mail;
Deeply the merciless foeman shall rue
    When on his ears shall ring,
    Borne on the breeze's wing,
Tir Connell's dread war-cry, 'O'Donnell Aboo!'

Wildly o'er Desmond the war-wolf is howling,
Fearless the eagle sweeps over the plain,
The fox in the streets of the city is prowling;
All, all who would scare them are banished or slain.
    Grasp every stalwart hand
    Hackbut and battle brand,
Pay them all back the debt so long due;
    Norris and Clifford well
    Can of Tir Connell tell;
Onward to glory, 'O'Donnell Aboo!'

Sacred the cause of Clan Conaill defending,
The altars we kneel at, the homes of our sires;
Ruthless the ruin the foe is extending,
Midnight is red with the plunderers' fires.
    On with O'Donnell, then,
Fight the old fight again
Sons of Tir Connell, all valiant and true.
    Make the false Saxon feel
    Erin's avenging steel;
Strike for your country, 'O'Donnell Aboo!'

Eithne

Seumas MacManus

Seumas MacManus was born in Inver in 1869 and became a teacher and writer of folktales which found a ready market in America. In 1901 he married Anna Johnston who wrote poetry as Ethna Carbery but she died only a year later. This poem is a tribute to her. He died in the USA in 1960.

The pleasant paths your feet had blessed
    Beneath our changing sky,
The flower-swept brae, the flame-struck moor,
    You left without good-bye –

And the linnet's plaintive pipe,
    And throstle's cheery call
That charmed your soul, through days of bliss,
    In glens of Donegal:

You left the fond Hills of your Heart
    Where love's bright bow found birth;
And one you left who loved you, Love,
    Above all things on earth.

But now, your linnet always lilts,
    Your throstle ever trills,
Where you uplift a radiant face
    Amid eternal hills –

Through mazes of unending bliss
    Down glens of joy you glide –
Would God your hand were held in mine,
    And I walked by your side.

By the Short Cut to the Rosses
Nora Hopper

Nora Hopper was born in Exeter in 1871, the daughter of an army captain.
She was friendly with Yeats and George Moore, and died in 1906.

By the short cut to the Rosses,
    A fairy girl I met;
I was taken by her beauty
    Just like fishes in the net.
The fern uncurled to look at her
    So very fair was she,
With her hair as bright as seaweed
    That floats in from the sea.

By the short cut to the Rosses,
    'Twas on the first of May,
I heard the fairies piping,
    And they piped my heart away;
They piped 'till I was mad with joy,
    But when I was alone,
I found my heart was piped away –
    And in my breast, a stone.

By the short cut to the Rosses,
    'Tis I'll go never more,
Lest she should also steal my soul,
    Who stole my heart before.
Lest she should take my soul and crush it,
    Like a dead leaf in her hand,
For the short cut to the Rosses
    Is the way to fairyland.

HERE AND THERE

Loch Salt in Donegal
from *Sketches in Ireland*
Caesar Otway

Caesar Otway was born in Tipperary in 1780 and became a clergyman. He was William Carleton's first publisher in his mainly proselytising magazine the *Christian Examiner*. He died in Dublin in 1842.

Ascending the steep side of the Kilmacaennan Mountain, we at length reached the top of the mountain (or rather the summit of the pass through the 'ridge'), and suddenly turning the point of a cliff that jutted out and checked the road, we came abruptly into a hollow something like the crater of an extinct volcano, which was filled almost entirely by a lovely lake, on the right hand of which rose the high peak of the mountain, so bare, so serrated, so tempest-worn, so vexed at the storms of the Atlantic, that if matter could suffer we might suppose that this lofty and precipitous peak presented the appearance of material endurance: not one tint of shadowing that decks and paints a mountain brow was wanting. Here was the brown heath, grey lichen, green fern, and red cranesbill; and there, down the face of the cliff, from the top to the water's edge, the black, seared streak of a meteoric stone, which had shattered itself against the crest of the mountain, and rolled down in fiery fragments into the lake, was distinctly visible. On the other side, a fair, verdant bank presented itself, courting the traveller to take rest; gentle and grassy knolls were here and there interspersed, on which sheep of a most picturesque leanness – some black, some white – were grazing. But the lake! Not a breath was abroad on its expanse; it smiled as it reflected the grey mountain and the azure face of heaven; it seemed as if on this day the spirit of the Atlantic had fallen asleep, and air, and earth, and ocean were celebrating the festival of repose; the waters of the lake, of the colour and clearness of the sky, were : *Blue, darkly, deeply, beautifully blue.* You could look down a hundred fathoms deep and see no bottom. Speckled trout, floating at immense depths, seemed as if they soared in ether. Then the stillness of the scene: you seemed lifted, as it were, out of the turmoil of the world into some planetary paradise.

Donegal Customs
From *Dairies* (1849)
William Allingham

Allingham's diaries in three volumes are now read with greater interest than most of his poetry. His work as a customs officer (from 1846 till 1870) meant that he travelled widely about what were then called the British Isles.

Monday, 1 January. Donegal – Write on slavery. Black v. White (is writing for pay advisable?) Walk to mill. Hungry – dinner – violin, Tennyson's poems. Reverend Jos. Welsh and English land-agent Wilson, after attending investigation into the Wray explosion, came to a snack in my room. Wilson looked into my Tennyson, and, saying, 'Now this is what I call *stuff!*' began to read out part of 'Oenone'. I said, 'Let me look at it,' and put the book in my pocket without another word. He appeared rather stunned. How Tennyson gives the effect of everything – enriched with a peculiar glow! Violin again.

Friday, 5 January. Frost. Customs accounts. To Killybegs by Mail-Car, walk up the long hills, slip on skates and skate a little by the roadside, then run after the car, warm. Denis laughing.

Inver. Sun sinking, deep red globe with a stroke of black cloud in the centre; now an arch, as it were the open gate of Heaven revealing glory within; now a ruby moon; now the last look from a deep eye of radiance, and – all's gone.

Wrote 'Crucible'. Read aloud.

8 January. At Killybegs. Read Tennyson and Wittick's *Norway. Fairy Song*: 'Wee folk, good folk[1],' [see p. 23] etc. Violin.

Thursday, 15 March. Ballyshannon. Plant ivy round the Old Barrack ruins, accompanied by three pairs of slate castanets. Walk through fields at Coolcolly, with sycamores, green mounds, and rillet hid within a hedge, a place of mysterious beauty to me in old old days of childhood; and so across the Abbey river, around Legaltion Lough, and home. Mem: the word 'brook' not used here: they say 'river' or 'water'; and 'water' is also applied to large streams. After dinner down the Mall; boys with hoops leaping wall. Aboard *Kent*. Sailors on boat, a coarse and reckless set.

People catching young eels (*lifogues*) no thicker than twine, in bags; they are cooked into the shape of cakes or small cheeses. But this catching of the fry is not allowed. Tea. French.

Mr Heagney (the Collector) remarks on hearing of the death of a retired Customs officer whom he knew, 'It's a queer world this! There's a man gone that had eleven and eightpence a day – eleven and eightpence! I wonder where Moses and Aaron are now, and David and Goliath, and all these. They were certainly here – they certainly were. And Nero and Caligula too – bad, bad men, tyrants – tye-ranny – tye-rrannous! – not a chirp in them!' Some ships were waiting in the bay for a chance of crossing the bar. I asked, 'Will they get in today?' Mr H. (ironically), 'Ay! – there's a line of breakers as white as Ananias's wall at Jerusalem, and the Alps and Apennines beyond them. Get in!'

Sunday, 24 June. Ballyshannon. Have been appointed Controller of Customs at Ramsey, Isle of Man, at £120 a year. Letter today ordering me to go. Last Sunday here – for how long?

The Nameless Doon
William Larminie

William Larminie was born in Castlebar in 1849 and was for many years a civil servant. He died in 1900. The 'doon' is that in Lough Doon, near Portnoo.

Who were the builders? Question not the silence
That settles on the lake for evermore,
Save when the sea-bird screams and to the islands
The echo answers from the steep-cliffed shore.
O half-remaining ruin, in the lore
Of human life a gap shall all deplore
Beholding thee; since thou art like the dead
Found slain, no token to reveal the why,
The name, the story. Some one murdered
We know, we guess; and gazing upon thee
And, filled by thy long silence of reply,
We guess some garnered sheaf of tragedy; –
Of tribe or nation slain so utterly
That even their ghosts are dead, and on their grave
Springeth no bloom of legend in its wildness;
And age by age weak washing round the islands
No faintest sigh of story lisps the wave.

At the Turn o' the Road

Elizabeth Shane (1877-1951)

Loughanure is two miles from Annagry and on the main road between Crolly
and Dungloe. The 'great big stone', an ice-age erratic, was a popular meeting
place about a quarter of a mile from Crolly.

As I was comin' from Lough Anure
    Wi' sheep for the fair at Annagrey,
Near Crolly town, at the turn o' the road
    Where the big grey stone is beside the way,
I met the one I had never seen,
    An' she broke my luck for the fair that day.

There's girls I like in the country-side,
    Round Lough Anure an' away to Dore;
But the one that stood by the owld grey stone
    I never had seen her like before.
'God save you now, sure you're strange,' said I,
    'But you're welcome here for it all the more.'

Her dark hair shone wi' a glint o' gold
    Like the sun's own light on a turfy stream,
An' her eyes were stormy clouds o' grey
    Lit up by the flash o' a lightenin' gleam.
She said no word, an' it moithered me
    For fear she mightn't be what she'd seem.

'Now let you be o' the fairy folk
    An' I'll have luck if I sell or buy;
An' let you be e'er a witch itself
    I can but take to my heels an' fly;
Or let you be but a livin' girl
    An' sure I could like you well,' said I.

She looked at me like a frightened hare
    An' through the heather she leaped away.
Och! How could I think to sell or buy
    Or take the fun o' the fair that day?
I drove my sheep to the hills again
    An' bad luck followed me all the way.

There's girls I like in the country side
    By Lough Anure an Crolly an' Dore,
An' why would it be that my heart would go
    To one I never had seen before?
An' her that hadn't a word to say,
An' me that never might see her more.

An' sure if I go Crolly now,
    Whenever I pass the owld grey stone
At the turn o' the road, I'll think I see
    The shape o' her standin' there, ochone!
Wi' her troubled eyes an' her shinin' hair
There's not the like o' her anywhere;
An', though where to find her there's none can tell,
I know in my heart I like her well
    Och! It's hard to thravel the world alone.

My Lagan Love

Joseph Campbell

Where Lagan stream sings lullaby,
    There blows a lily fair.
The twilight is in her eye,
    The night is on her hair.
And, like a lovesick leananshee,
    She hath my heart in thrall.
Nor life I own, nor liberty,
    For love is lord of all.

And often when the beetle's horn
    Hath lulled the eve to sleep;
I steal unto her shieling lorn,
    And thro' the dooring peep.
There in the crickets' singing-stone
    She stirs the bogwood fire,
And hums in sad sweet undertone,
    The song of heart's desire.

Her welcome, like her love for me,
    Is from the heart within;
Her warm kiss is felicity,
That knows no taint or sin.
When she was only fairly small
Her gentle mother died,
But true love keeps her memory warm
    By Lagan's silver side.

Going Home
Patrick MacGill

'Going Home' comes from the repertoire of the 'Navvy Poet'.

I'm going back to Glenties when the harvest fields are brown,
And the Autumn sunset lingers on my little Irish town;
    When the gossamer is shining where the moorland
        blossoms blow
    I'll take the road across the hills I tramped so long ago –
'Tis far I am beyond the seas, but yearning voices call,
'Will you not come back to Glenties, and your wave-washed
    Donegal?'

I've seen the hopes of childhood stifled by the hand of time;
I've seen the smile of innocence become the frown of crime;
    I've seen the wrong rise high and strong; I've seen the fair
        betrayed,
    Until the faltering heart fell low the brave became afraid –
But still the cry comes out to me, the homely voices call,
From the Glen among the highlands of my ancient Donegal.

Sure, I think I see them often, when the night steals o'er the
    town,
The Braes of old Strasala, and the homes of Carrigdoun –
    There's a light in Jimmy Lynch's house, a shadow on the
        blind.
    I often watched the shadow, for 'twas Mary in behind.
And often in the darkness, 'tis myself that sees it all,

For I cannot help but dreaming of the folk in Donegal.
So I'll hie me back to Glenties when the harvest comes again,
And the kine are in the pasture and the berries in the lane,
Then they'll give me such a welcome that my heart will
leap for joy,
When my father and my mother welcome back their
wayward boy.
So I'm going back to Glenties when the autumn showers fall,
And the harvest home is cheery in my dear old Donegal.

FARE YE WELL

The Hills of Donegal

Anonymous

Oh, Donegal, the pride of all, my heart still turns to thee,
My cottage home, where oft I've roamed when I was young
    and free.
Big houses grand in a foreign land cannot compare at all
To my cottage bright on a winter's night on the hills of
    Donegal.

Right well I mind the harvest time, that doleful dreary day,
When I left all in Donegal to wander far away.
Near Creeslough town my friends stood roun'; I bid farewell
    to all,
And from the van I waved my han' to the hills of Donegal.

Gazing back through Barnesgap on my own native hill,
I thought no shame (oh, who could blame) 'twas there I cried
    my fill.
My parents kind ran in my mind, my friends and comrades all –
My heart did ache, I thought 'twould break, in leaving Donegal.

From Derry Quay we steamed away, the waters calm and still;
Down Lough Foyle our tug did toil to the big ship at Moville.
Some love to see each tower and tree, each ancient lordly hall,
But my thoughts that day were far away on the hills of
    Donegal.

Round Tory Isle we steamed in style, the mainland we could
   see,
Tall Muckish grand, with glistening sand, smile over
   Cruckatee;
Elagh much more brighter still, looked proudly over all;
I heaved a sigh and bid good-bye to the hills of Donegal.

Among those hills St Columbkille left miracles and cures,
Amid streams and dells and holy wells his power it still
   endures;
Green Gartan cell and the old Doon Well, where St Finian's
   waters fall
A simple shrine unchanged by time on the hills of Donegal.

Oh, Donegal I long to see your native hills once more,
As I am now an exile upon a foreign shore,
Whenever I return again I'll build a castle tall,
And live where my forefathers lived, and die in Donegal.

––––––––––––––

Mary from Dungloe

Anonymous

––––––––––––––

Oh, then, fare ye well, sweet Donegal, the Rosses and Gweedore.
I'm crossing the main ocean, where the foaming billows roar.
It breaks my heart from you to part, where I spent many
   happy days
Farewell to kind relations, for I'm bound for Amerikay.

Oh, my love is tall and handsome and her age is scarce
    eighteen;
She far exceeds all other fair maids when she trips over the
    green;
Her lovely neck and shoulders are fairer than the snow.
Till the day I die I'll ne'er deny my Mary from Dungloe.

If I was at home in Sweet Dungloe a letter I would write;
Kind thoughts would fill my bosom for Mary my delight;
'Tis in her father's garden, the fairest violets grow
And 'twas there I came to court the maid, my Mary from
    Dungloe.

Ah then, Mary, you're my heart's delight my pride and only
    care,
It was your cruel father would not let me stay there.
But absence makes the heart grow fond and when I'm o'er
    the main
May the Lord protect my darling girl till I return again.

And I wish I was in Sweet Dungloe and seated on the grass
And by my side a bottle of wine and on my knee a lass.
I'd call for liquor of the best and I'd pay before I would go
And I'd roll my Mary in my arms in the town of Sweet
    Dungloe.

Duffy's Farewell
John Duffy

John Duffy came from Newmills, Letterkenny and wrote this piece on his own leaving c1890. The answer to the charade in the last verse is 'Catherine Broadly'.

Adieu, ye bonny winding banks,
    That border 'round Lough Swilly shore;
Of them I take a long farewell;
    I fear I'll never see them more.
While life remains I'll bear in mind
    The pleasant scenes from them I saw,
I soon must cross the Atlantic main
    To freedom's land that's far awa'.

Our good ship lies in readiness,
    At Londonderry, just beside,
May Providence our pilot be,
    And send a prosperous wind and tide.
My fortune I am bound to try
    In famous free Columbia,
When I think long, with brandy strong,
    I'll drown all care when far awa'.

It grieves my youthful tenderness,
    The leaving of my native shore;
Besides, to think that I must part

With the handsome maid that I adore.
My heart with love is sore oppressed,
   Since first her lovely face I saw;
She's my delight, both day and night,
   And ever will when I'm awa'.

With sweethearts, friends and comrades,
   Oh, many's the happy days I spent,
With jovial mirth and revelry,
   I spent my youthful days content.
But now Oppression's cruel chains,
   Which does, indeed, surround us a',
It makes me weep, when I should sleep,
   In a foreign clime, when far awa'.

Farewell to Convoy and Raphoe,
   Ramelton and Rathmullan, too,
Kirkneedy, and old Roohan braes,
   Unto them all I bid adieu.
Sweet Letterkenny I must leave,
   Where many's the blooming girl I saw,
And while I ride the winding tide,
   I'll sigh for them when far awa'.

Her name to trace, a beast first place
   A river next you may transpose,
And what the vast Atlantic is
   With fifty, and a vowel shows.
This beauty she has jet black eyes,
   I love her I make bold to say;
Alas! I cannot count my sighs,
   Since she can't come to Amerikay.

A Scene in the South
From *The Irish People and the Irish Land*
Isaac Butt

Isaac Butt was born in Cloghan near Fintown in 1813 and after strong support for unionism changed to become the leader of the Irish party. He lost the position with the coming of Parnell. He died in 1879 and was buried, according to his stated wish, in Stranorlar.

Let me say once for all how I came to write. Two year ago I had formed views of the land question, as, I suppose, most persons in my position have. I was satisfied of that which lies on the very surface – that insecurity of tenure is a great evil. I was convinced that compensation for tenants' improvements was just and right; but when I saw people flying in masses from their homes I felt that really to understand the question we must go deeper that all this – that there must be some mischief deeply rooted in our social system, which in a country blessed with advantages like ours produced results so strangely contrary to everything which the laws which regulate the history of nations or the conduct of classes or individuals might lead us to expect.

An accident turned my thoughts more intensely in this direction. Travelling on the Southern railway, I witnessed one of those scenes too common in our country, but which, I believe, no familiarity can make any person of feeling witness without emotion. The station was crowded with emigrants and their friends who came to see them off. There was nothing unusual in the occurrence – nothing that is not often to be seen. Old men walked slowly, and almost hesitatingly, to the carriages that were to take them away from the country to which they were never to return. Railway porters placed in the train strange boxes and chests of every shape and size, sometimes even small articles of furniture, which told that the owners were taking with them their little all. In the midst of them a brother and a sister bade each other their last farewell – a mother clasped passionately to her breast the son whom she must never see again. Women carried or led to their places in the carriages little children, who looked round as if they knew not what all this meant, but wept because they saw their mothers weeping. Strong men turned aside to dash from their eye the not unmanly tear. As the train began to move there was the uncontrollable rush, the desperate clinging to the carriages of relatives crowding down to give the last shake-hands. The railway servants pushed them back – we moved on more rapidly – and then rose from the group we left behind a strange mingled cry of wild farewells, and prayers, and blessings, and that melancholy wail of Irish sorrow which no one who has heard will ever forget – and we rushed on with our freight of sorrowing and reluctant exiles across a plain of fertility unsurpassed, perhaps, in any European soil. It was a light matter, but still there is something in that picture – close to us rose the picturesque ruins which seemed to tell us from the past that there were days when an Irish race had lived, and not lived in poverty, upon that very plain.

These are scenes which surely no Irishman should see without emotion. The transient feeling they may excite is but of little use except as it may be suggestive of thought. It was impossible not to ask why were these people thus flying from their homes, deserting that rich soil. I could not but feel that no satisfactory solution of the question had yet been given. I asked myself if it was not a reproach to those amongst us whom God had raised a little above that people by the advantages of intellect and education if we gave no real earnest thought to such an inquiry; and I formed a purpose – I almost made to myself a vow – that I would employ, as far as I could, what ever little power I had acquired in investigating facts in endeavouring to trace the strange mystery of its origin.

Mary of Carrick
Ethna Carbery

Mary of Carrick has gone away
From our pleasant places, down to the sea,
She has put a loss on our mountain grey,
She has drained the joy from the heart o' me,
        Mary a-stór,
        Mary a-stór,
Black hair, black eyes, I am grieving sore!

Mary of Carrick is small and sweet –
My Share of the World how sweet were you
Tripping along on the little bare feet
With your milking-pails through the rainbow dew?
        Mary a-stór,
        Mary a-stór,
The sun was a shadow with you to the fore!

Mary of Carrick gave only a smile –
No word of comfort for words I spake,

But since she has left me, this weary while,
My heart is learning the way to break,
> *Mary a-stór,*
> *Mary a-stór,*
Quick is my learning – and bitter the lore!

Mary of Carrick 'tis you I must follow,
For where you are 'tis there I must be –
On mountain grey, or in heathery hollow,
Or where the salt wind blows from the sea
> *Mary a-stór*
> *Mary a-stór*
When I find I shall bind you, nor lose evermore!

The Emigrant's Letter
Percy French

Percy French was born in Cloonyquin, County Roscommon in 1854. After being 'Inspector of Drains' for Co Cavan he began a full time career as humorist, travelling entertainer and superb writer of Irish songs. He died in Formby, Lancashire in 1920. The germ of this piece was a remark overheard by him and his partner, Houston Collisson, on their first voyage to America.

Dear Danny,
I'm takin' the pen in me hand
To tell you we're just out of sight of the land;
In the grand Allen liner we're sailin' style
But we're sailin' away from the Emerald Isle;

And a long sort of sigh seemed to rise from us all
As the waves hid the last bit of ould Donegal.
Och! it's well to be you that is takin' yer tay
Where they're cuttin' the corn in Creeshla the day.

I spoke to the captain – he won't turn her round,
And if I swum back I'd be apt to be drowned;
I'll stay where I am, for the diet is great,
The best of combustibles piled on me plate
But though it is 'sumpchus', I'd swop the whole lot
For the ould wooden spoon and the stirabout pot,
And Katey foreninst me a-wettin' the tay
Where they're cuttin' the corn in Creeshla the day!

There's a woman on board who knows Katey by sight;
So we talked of old times till they put out the light
I'm to meet the good woman tomorra on deck
And we'll talk about Katey from this to Quebec.
I know I'm no match for her – oh! not the least,
With her house and two cows, and her brother a priest
But the woman declares Katey's heart on the say
And mine's back with Katey in Creeshla the day.

If Katey is courted by Patsey or Mick
Put a word in for me with a lump of a stick;
Don't kill Patsey outright; he had no sort of chance,
But Mickey's a rogue you might murdher at wance;
For Katey might think, as the longer she waits,
A boy in the hand is worth two in the States:
And she'll promise to honour, to love and obey
Some robber that's roamin' round Creeshla the day.

Goodbye to you, Dan, there's no more to be said,
And I think the salt wather's got into me head,
For it dreeps from my eyes when I call to me mind
The friends and the colleen I'm leavin' behind;
But still she might wait; whin I bid her goodbye
There was just the last taste of a tear in her eye,
And a break in her voice whin she said, 'You might stay;
But plaze God you'll come back to ould Creeshla some day.'

———————

Farewell to Donegal
Seumas MacManus (1869-1960)

———————

The big ship she lies waitin',
    And manned by all her hands,
To hoist the sail by the mornin's gale,
    And off to foreign lands.
Soon we must sigh a sad good-bye,
    To friends and kindred all.
To the homes we love, and the hills above,
    In dear old Donegal!
      In dear old Donegal!
      In loved old Donegal!
To the homes we love, and the hills above,
    In dear old Donegal!

Oft through her glens we've wandered,
    We've roamed along her hills,
When skies were bright, and young hearts light
    And wayward as her rills;
But dire misfortunes gathered since
    And to our lot did fall,
'Tis why we go, with load of woe,
    From dear old Donegal,
        From dear old Donegal!
        From loved old Donegal!
'Tis why we go with load of woe,
    From dear old Donegal!

The boys and girls will joyful join
    The dance upon the green,
With song and shout, and laugh rung out,
    And maybe a tear between:
Och, they'll keep it up till the stars come forth
    And the white lights on them fall;
And all the while we're many a mile
    From the hills of Donegal,
        Of dear old Donegal!
        Of loved old Donegal!
And all the while we're many a mile
    From the hills of Donegal!

There's Teague and Ted, and Paddy's Ned,
    And Micky Roe and I,
Will everyone, ere the morrow's sun,
    Have bade you a last good-bye;
Och! sore 'twill grieve our hearts, to leave
    The hill where curlews call,

And fairy rings where the blackbird sings
    All day in Donegal,
     In dear old Donegal!
       In loved old Donegal!
And fairy rings where the blackbird sings
    All day in Donegal!

Farewell to the heathery mountains,
    And farewell to the pleasant vales,
To the flashing rills from the grey old hills,
    That sweep adown the dales,
To the boys so rare, and the cailíns fair –
    'Tis fare-ye-well to all!
For God knows when we'll meet again
    In dear old Donegal!
       In dear old Donegal!
       In loved old Donegal!
Och, God knows when we'll meet again
    In dear old Donegal!

INDEX OF AUTHORS AND POETS

INDEX OF TITLES AND FIRST LINES OF POEMS